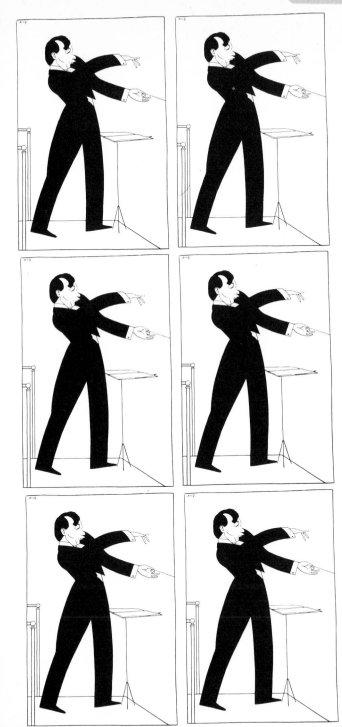

The performing world of the musician

The performing world of the musician

Christopher Headington

with a profile of
Andrew Lloyd Webber

Hamish Hamilton
London

to Ed Welch

Designed and produced by Breslich & Foss, London

Design: Leslie & Lorraine Gerry
Picture Research: Mary Corcoran
House Editor: Timothy Roberts
Interviews with Andrew Lloyd Webber and Sue Addison: Pamela Harvey
Interview with Jerry Harrison: Deborah Waroff

First published in 1981
by Hamish Hamilton Children's Books
Garden House 57–59 Long Acre London WC2E 9JZ

British Library Cataloguing in Publication Data

   Headington, Christopher
   The performing world of the musician.
   1. Music—Juvenile literature
   I. Title
   780   ML3930.A2

   ISBN 0–241–10587–0

Printed in Great Britain
by BAS Printers Limited, Over Wallop, Hampshire
and bound by Leighton Straker

Contents

The Minstrel's Art

1

Performer and Audience

Players of musical instruments have been valued by all societies throughout history. A thousand years before Christ, the future King David played his lyre to cure the disturbed mood of Saul. In the mid-eighteenth century J. S. Bach astounded King Frederick the Great by his keyboard improvisation. In the early nineteenth century the violin virtuoso Paganini toured Europe and drove audiences wild with his playing, surrounded himself with legend, and earned huge sums of money. The status of the Romantic virtuoso was such that the Polish pianist Paderewski was actually elected prime minister of Poland in 1919. In our time, the great Russian pianist Vladimir Horowitz emerged from semi-retirement to give a televised concerto performance in the USA for which he earned around a quarter of a million dollars.

Horowitz, of course, is no ordinary pianist. A paid performer must be in a totally different class from the amateur who plays at home but does not demonstrate his skill before a paying audience. He is, after all, a professional. More than this, Horowitz is a virtuoso, a 'star' performer of exceptional technical attainment. As a young man he was for piano playing what Pele has been to football or Bjorn Borg to tennis. Now, in his seventies, he is even more of a legend; for unlike sportsmen who must see their skill decline

Vladimir Horowitz, a living legend among pianists

with age, a musician can retain his dexterity almost indefinitely. There is also a feeling that the older artist has acquired a kind of wisdom that is reflected in his playing. Several conductors have been active right into their eighties; and Leopold Stokowski was conducting before large audiences when over ninety!

What is the nature of the performer's skill? First of all he must entertain his audience. He does so by the quality and energy of his playing, like the footballer or tennis player. But while there are many different kinds of football game, requiring different strategies, at least the rules do not change and the pitch remains the same size and shape. The musician, however, must be wider ranging. If he is a violinist, he may one day play unaccompanied J. S. Bach, the next day he may play Beethoven in a string quartet, and go on to perform a modern violin concerto with an orchestra; and he might also do recording 'sessions' of pop and light music. Each of these musical activities involves a different musical 'language', a different sound from his instrument, even a physically different technique

2

of bowing and fingering. A musician, like an actor, must have *range*, both technically and imaginatively.

Yehudi Menuhin rehearses a concerto

Imagination is important. A performing musician stands before the music and turns it into sound. All he has to go on is a set of instructions, in what is called musical notation; but that is not the actual music any more than a recipe for an omelette is the finished dish. The performer therefore creates—or at least, recreates. And of course, a minstrel, folk or jazz musician who really invents the music is a creator in a fuller sense. What a folk or jazz performer usually does is to play existing tunes his own way— and the tunes are not written down for him as they would be for a 'classical' musician performing in a concert. He is more like the story-tellers that still exist in Arab countries and elsewhere: the tale they tell is probably entirely familiar, but it is told in their own words. The blend of familiarity and newness is important. Whether in the folk or 'classical' tradition, it is the performer who brings that individuality which makes every performance different.

To appreciate the varied qualities of imagination that a performer needs, suppose that a violinist like Yehudi Menuhin is giving a recital. He may begin with Bach and then go on to a sonata by Mozart or

3

Beethoven; after the interval it will probably be Romantic music and perhaps a piece by a twentieth-century composer like Bartók; and then there will be the 'lollipops', the lighter short piece or two given as encores. Now all these pieces of music are quite different, for the composers lived in different countries during many different periods of history. But the performer must 'get inside' each piece in turn to bring it to life from the printed 'score', that set of instructions left by a composer perhaps long dead. He must almost *become* each composer in turn to recreate their music. Performance can be thrilling and satisfying—and exhausting, too. The famous French actor Jean-Louis Barrault said that playing the part of Shakespeare's Hamlet made him ill: 'One loses two pounds in weight every evening: if one starts too fast one runs the risk of collapsing at the end . . . yet however frightened I might be by Hamlet, I love him as an eldest brother: he is somebody who is alive and who exists.' The English pianist John Lill has said that when he plays a Beethoven sonata he actually feels the presence of the composer.

A final point has to do with sheer enjoyment. The performer has to like what he is doing—appearing before that particular audience, playing his instrument, and enjoying the music he plays. If it gives him no pleasure, it can hardly give much to his listeners. They give him their attention, and their money too; and in return they expect to enjoy themselves. A performer is conscious of his audience, of its moods and needs, and responds to them.

Fortunately not every performer is expected to go so far as the unfortunate young player of the double pipe whose story was told by the Greek writer Lucian in the second century A.D. His name was Harmonides and he was making his début at a competitive festival. Determined to astonish the judges and the audience, he 'began his solo with so violent a blast' that he died on the spot! Poor Harmonides must hold the record for the shortest musical career in history.

The Ancient World

Harmonides belonged to the world of the ancient Greeks. It was an age that was rich in music. Without mass entertainment (like today's recordings and television) and with very few able to read, the musical performer was greatly valued. Indeed every ancient society had some sort of music. The Egyptians had wind instruments, plucked string instruments and percussion, and fourteen centuries before Christ they buried a trumpet in King Tutankhamun's tomb. The Chinese also valued music—flutes, drums, bells and even temple orchestras with plucked string instruments. In the home or the temple musicians were always desirable. In Confucius's words, 'the music of a man of noble mind is gentle and delicate, enlivens and moves.' The ancient Indians, while preferring the human voice in worship, liked also to employ instrumentalists for dancing and other entertainments.

This fifteenth-century illustration shows King David and his choir. King David is known to have been a gifted musician

Musicians played an important part in early Jewish history, in that part of the world which gave birth to Christianity. Their greatest early leader, Moses, was trained in music by the Egyptians, among whom he lived as a boy. The Bible tells us (in *Numbers* 10) that God instructed him in the making of trumpets, silver instruments used for signalling. The boy David played the *kinnor*, a lyre; in later life

5

he is said to have taken his instrument with him when travelling and in *Chronicles* we read that he gave the Levite tribe the responsibility of providing temple musicians. His son, King Solomon, had 'musical instruments, and that of all sorts'. These instruments were common to other countries like Egypt and Babylonia: in *Daniel* 3 the band of King Nebuchadnezzar of Babylonia is described, and these court musicians were presumably full-time professionals—in the sixth century B.C.! By Christ's time the Jewish temple orchestra had nine lyres, two harps and cymbals. The Jews also used the double pipe, or *halil*, associated with exciting entertainment or dancing rather than solemn temple rituals. But they gave up the use of temple instruments after they lost their homeland. As for the Christians, in time they too turned away from the musical performers' exciting arts. Two centuries after Christ, the Christian philosopher Clement of Alexandria said that the faithful should no longer seek the sound of the 'trumpet, drum and flute, liked by those who prepare war'.

Greece and Rome

Greek music had its origins at least partly from Egypt, via the island of Crete. But the greatest minstrel of Greek legend, Orpheus, came from Thrace in the north-east of the country, and his singing, which he accompanied on the lyre, was said to charm wild beasts, trees and even rocks. This music was essentially soothing and Orpheus (who may have been a real person) has always been thought of as a

Orpheus, the legendary Greek minstrel, charms the animals (some also legendary, like the unicorn) and birds with his music

peacemaker. The other main Greek instrument, besides the lyre, was a double-reed wind instrument called the *aulos*; it sounded much wilder and was associated with the cult of the god Dionysus. It was played by brilliant professional players at competitive festivals. The earliest known piece of 'programme', or descriptive, music was performed by a player called Sakados in 586 B.C., at the Pythian Games held at Delphi: it depicted a fight between Apollo and a dragon (won by the god, of course).

The Greek philosophers—especially Plato—accorded music a high place in education. But in the fourth century B.C. Aristotle warned against brilliant performance for its own sake, saying that music students should 'stop short of the arts practised in professional contests . . . those fantastic marvels of performance which are now the fashion.' Later it became rare for the educated classes to have much to do with music. However in the Roman Empire, of which Greece eventually became a part, both professional and amateur performance flourished. In A.D. 60 the Emperor Nero founded a series of music festivals at which he himself performed on the *kithara*, the Greek lyre, and like other players he would follow the etiquette of the occasion and address his audience politely ('kindly pay me your benevolent attention'), though anyone caught being inattentive incurred his displeasure and perhaps worse. Nero probably did not 'fiddle while Rome burned', as the tale has it; but his dying words are supposed to have been 'What an artist is lost in me!' As for the real professionals, they could live well if they had influential friends. It seems that some players were willing to sell their affections for large sums, and in the second century the wife of the Emperor Pertinax caused a scandal by her love affair with a lyre player. The notorious Emperor Caligula took musicians with him when he travelled, even on board ship, as did others of high rank and wealth; the musicians would have been skilled slaves of his household. Dinner parties, too, were not complete without music. The essayist Pliny the Younger offered his guests a choice between a lecture and lyre playing (most people probably preferring the music), while his friend, the poet Martial, once apologized for providing a frugal meal but laid on some *aulos* playing in compensation. Towards the end of the Roman Empire, its eastern capital Byzantium boasted a court orchestra; there were organists too, playing instruments made with silver or even gold.

The Middle Ages

After Rome fell to the Vandals in the fifth century, western Europe lost its central government. But performers continued to make a living from music. Many took to the roads that were part of Rome's legacy, and became wandering minstrels. A lyre was easy enough to carry, and when it eventually wore out or broke another simpler instrument might be made from whatever materials were around. The same was true of the various wind instruments or pipes. Playing in a village was, of course, very different from entertaining Roman dinner guests; often it was dance music that was needed and drums, cymbals, tambourines and castanets were the order of the day. Percussion instruments do in fact feature in many musical pictures and carvings from around the eighth century.

In A.D. 800 the Frankish King Charlemagne was crowned Holy Roman Emperor by the Pope. It was the Christian Church that had largely held Europe together after Rome's fall, and monks had kept alive certain musical skills such as organ playing, though church music was now almost entirely vocal. Around 900, in the Netherlands, a monk called Hucbald expressed his admiration for the skill of 'lyre players and other secular musicians'. Again, these performers might be itinerant and independent, or might be attached to a court. The Crusades, between 1096 and 1291, produced tales of heroic deeds that could be sung, and there were noble minstrels in Southern France called troubadours. The poorer wandering musicians, skilled all-rounders whose French name *jongleur* means 'juggler', gradually became more organized, and by the eleventh century they had their own guilds. In twelfth-century Germany they had to 'play the drum, cymbals and hurdy-gurdy, to throw small apples and catch knives, perform card tricks and jump through hoops ... and play many other instruments'; but little by little the professional

Fourteenth-century
German minstrels play
the (plucked) psaltery
and the fiddle

skilled musical performer was emerging. The Welsh
minstrels, or bards, held contests for harpists and
lyre players, for bagpipers too—forerunners of
present-day eisteddfods (Welsh song festivals). In
England, too, minstrels were an accepted part of
daily life, and the kings Alfred the Great and
Richard the Lionheart were both musicians. But a
later king, Edward II, had to issue a decree in 1315
restraining performers from arriving uninvited at
houses or castles, expecting food, drink and *gyftes*—
that is, payment.

Musicians now had something like a profession,
but it did not have the status of a learned subject like
law or philosophy. A musician was more like a
skilled servant whose task was to entertain—though
in educated hands music might be refined and subtle.
Musical education was haphazard; a father would
teach his son, so that a family tradition grew, or a
master might take on an apprentice. The musicians'
guilds with their competitions gave other opportunities to learn new tunes or new instruments. There
were string instruments (plucked or bowed, as well as
the dulcimer which was struck); there were flutes
and recorders, shawms (loud forerunners of the
oboe), trumpets and horns, and many small percussion instruments. (Big drums could not be carried

9

A sixteenth-century gathering of musicians, poets and craftsmen

around.) For performers close to a church, there was the organ (in England, from about the ninth century). A big organ at Winchester Cathedral had no less than four hundred pipes. The 'merry organ' which we find in Christmas carols, and also in Chaucer, expressed joy at festival time.

And people did find time and energy for festivals, Christian or otherwise. Life was hard and often dangerous, but there were moments to give thanks for a harvest, for rain after drought, or for a feast given by a local lord. What better way to relax than with music, for singing or dancing? Musical performers were needed, and were popular. The profession grew not only in numbers but also in power and prestige.

Church, Court and Concert Hall

2

Church Musicians

In the late Middle Ages and through the Renaissance and Baroque periods that followed (from the fifteenth to mid-eighteenth centuries), the Christian Church was the principal patron of music and the main employer of musicians. A wealthy nobleman might have court performers, but court appointments were few compared to church posts which existed in every town. In church, instrumental music was mainly restricted to the organ, at least until the sixteenth century. But organists found plenty to do. Their instrument had originated with the panpipes, a small instrument of great antiquity found in Greece, China and elsewhere and consisting of a set of pipes bound or glued together, each producing a different note: it survives as a peasant instrument in Romania today. The panpipes were blown by the player: but a mechanical organ, supplied with air pumped by water pressure, was invented around 250 B.C., while a real pneumatic organ with bellows is recorded in the second century A.D. The organ came to Europe before A.D. 800; some time later it often had several sets ('ranks') of pipes producing different sounds. By the sixteenth century there might be two or more keyboards (or 'manuals') and a pedal keyboard also. By the eighteenth century the instrument had developed still further and was to inspire a performer-composer of genius, J. S. Bach.

Girolamo Frescobaldi, the famous organist of St Peter's Cathedral in Rome during the early seventeenth century

The earliest important organists worked in Italy. Adrian Willaert (actually from the Netherlands) was a famous organist of St Mark's Cathedral in Venice, a huge building with two organs as well as two choirs. His Venetian pupil Andrea Gabrieli also worked there from 1566, and in his time strings and brass instruments were added to produce rich effects. Claudio Merulo was another famous organist at St Mark's; when he went to perform at St Peter's in Rome the audience was so large and so excited that it had to be restrained to avoid injury in the crush. The St Peter's organist Girolamo Frescobaldi was such a popular performer that he attracted audiences of up to thirty thousand. Such excitement may seem extraordinary nowadays, when we tend to associate the organ with sober, reflective music; but at that time people were thrilled by its brilliant effects — particularly in toccatas, virtuoso pieces that displayed the player's dexterity to the full.

Outside Italy, organ performers like Jan Sweelinck used not only to play for services but also gave recitals. In Amsterdam around 1600 Sweelinck played his own versions of folk songs and even dances at these concerts. In England, his friend John Bull (the composer of a tune that may be the ancestor of 'God Save the Queen') was just one of many fine keyboard players, and was so skilled an organist that it was said of him that 'The bull by force in field doth reign, but Bull by skill good will doth gain'. Bull became the organist of Antwerp Cathedral in Belgium in 1617, showing us that music was an international art long before today's effortless continental travel.

The English Court

Of course many performers found themselves serving both Church and State, perhaps as a musician at court: the blind Antonio Cabezón was one of these at the Spanish court, playing the organ in the imperial chapel and also the clavichord for the entertainment of the Empress Isabella. Every court had its musicians, often drawn from several European countries according to their reputation. For example, the English lute player and composer John Dowland served King Christian IV of Denmark for eight years (1598–1606) and was paid a salary corresponding to that of an admiral of the Danish fleet. It might seem surprising that he was in demand so far from home, but in fact he travelled a good deal, as did many other musicians, offering his skills to any suitable employer.

English musicians were in demand abroad partly because there was a strong tradition of music at court. In King Henry V's time (the early fifteenth century) a visiting foreigner spoke of 'blessed England, full of melody'. A century later Henry VIII played the recorder, flute and virginals and had a huge collection of instruments. His daughter Elizabeth I played both the lute and the virginals—'for a queen, very well', according to a courtier. Both her sister Mary Tudor and Mary, Queen of Scots also liked to play the virginals (a keyboard instrument with plucked strings, like a small harpsichord); and though they may not have been especially skilful performers their interest in music meant that professional performers found a place at court.

Open-air dancing at Greenwich in the time of King Henry VIII: on the left is the king himself

Henry Purcell, the
greatest musician of
Restoration England

Opposite: English
minstrels or 'waits',
with bagpipe, fiddle and
treble shawm. The
intention of this 1879
engraving was to evoke
the fifteenth century,
but the instruments are
far from authentic

A century later, the outstanding composer in
seventeenth-century English music was Henry Purcell (1659–95). His father and his uncle were court
musicians, and he was brought up as a choirboy. At
twenty he became the organist of Westminster Abbey
in London, and from that time on he was involved in
all sides of English musical life. Restoration England
had a young king, Charles II, who brought gaiety
back to the country after the rather gloomy Com-
monwealth period. Purcell was much involved in
theatre music, but he could when necessary produce
church music to the king's taste—though others
might shake their heads and speak of 'the French
fantastical light way, better suiting a tavern, or
playhouse, than a church'.

King Charles himself liked to sing to a guitar
accompaniment played by his brother James, the
future King James II. He also liked folk musicians, as
we learn from the diarist Samuel Pepys. There were

14

plenty of these. At St James's Fair each May (held in
the area of London now called Mayfair) there were
'the catterwauling scrapes of thrashing fiddlers, the
grumbling of beaten calves-skin, and the discording
toots of broken organs'. Pepys, like his king, cared

little for artificial distinctions between 'cultivated' and popular music, and liked to take part in amateur music-making in inns like *The Dolphin*, where he 'sang and sometimes fiddled', or *The Green Dragon* where he sang and played his recorder. Nowadays poor Mr Pepys would be thrown out for enjoying himself in that fashion.

Both in London and in the provinces there were also salaried municipal performers of music called waits. If the king or other important person travelled to a city like Norwich or Oxford, there were welcoming bands of shawms, trombones and other instruments whose loud music was suited to outdoor ceremonial occasions. They were trained musicians and perhaps members of guilds, conscious of their professional dignity and attired in expensive costumes. The father of the composer Orlando Gibbons was not only an Oxford wait but also a city councillor. Musical families tended to seek employment among the waits, and it was therefore entirely natural that the young Orlando Gibbons should have trained as a musician.

Composer and Performer

Nowadays we tend to regard the composer and performer as two distinct kinds of musician. In earlier times no such distinction existed, and composers, as well as writing down music for other people to play, were often also expected to be able to improvise music on the spot. Such improvisation is familiar to us in jazz today, and in the Baroque period (about 1600–1750) regular chord sequences were often used, particularly in dance music. The greatest players, though, were able to make up very elaborate music such as fugues—these were pieces in a strict number of parts or 'voices', all moving independently though 'conversing' with each other.

This tradition of improvisation has largely died out (except among organists). A concert pianist is expected to play every note of a Mozart piano concerto exactly as written—even though we know that Mozart himself was a great improviser and might have made small changes as he played it. On the other hand, composers these days are not expected to be able to make up music on the spot, or even to perform at all. The habit of improvisation perhaps explains how the composers of the Baroque managed to write so prolifically in lifetimes that were generally rather shorter than those of today. One of the greatest of all the composer-performers, J. S. Bach (1685–1750), wrote well over one thousand works in his forty-five years of adult life, as well as playing, organizing ensemble music, teaching—and fathering twenty children!

Bach the Performer

Bach belonged to a family which included numerous town musicians who in England would have been called waits. *Grove's Dictionary of Music and Musicians* lists no less than thirty-eight Bachs, the first of whom was born around 1520. One town, Erfurt, associated this family so firmly with music that they went on calling their town musicians 'Bachs' even when there was no longer anyone of that name employed. J. S. Bach, the greatest of the family, thus came from a totally musical background. From childhood he breathed music.

Bach's father taught him the violin and viola. Then, when he was nine, his father died and he went in 1695 to live with an elder brother who taught him musical theory and the keyboard instruments of the time: the organ, harpsichord and clavichord. He learned quickly, and was constantly asking for more difficult music to play. He walked thirty miles to Hamburg to hear the famous performer Reincken playing the organ. Back at home, he would go to improvise at his local church, filling it with cascades of sound, calm prayerful melodies or strange adventures into forbidden realms of harmony. At fifteen he left home to sing in a choir, and three years later joined the Duke of Weimar's court orchestra as a violinist. But he only stayed a few months and next took a post as a church organist at the smallish town of Arnstadt. After a couple of years he asked for a month's leave and took the opportunity to hear the celebrated player Dietrich Buxtehude at Lübeck, two hundred miles away to the north. Bach was thrilled. At over sixty Buxtehude was about to retire and Bach might have become his successor—except that a condition of the appointment was that he had to

J. S. Bach: master musician of the Baroque period

17

St Thomas's Church in
Leipzig, where
J. S. Bach directed the
music for nearly thirty
years

marry Buxtehude's daughter, a lady several years older than himself! Such were the problems facing a performer in the early eighteenth century. Bach went instead back to Arnstadt, where he was in disgrace for overstaying his leave. Inspired by his travels, he treated his congregation to 'wondrous variations and strange sounds' on the organ—which were not to provincial taste. A year later he took another post, at Mühlhausen.

In 1708, after only a year at Mühlhausen (where he had not had enough to live on), Bach went to serve the Duke of Weimar. The chapel was cold and the organ less good than at Mühlhausen, which had been improved under his own direction. Conditions in the musicians' gallery were cramped. But he stayed for nine years, and became increasingly famous as an organist. The future King Frederick I of Sweden was so impressed when he heard Bach in 1714 that he took a diamond ring from his finger and presented it to the musician.

Next came six years (1717–23) at the princely court of Cöthen where Bach wrote his famous Brandenburg Concertos. He then took his last and longest appointment as director of music at St Thomas's Church in Leipzig. He was now eminent and much in demand in neighbouring cities to give recitals or to advise on organ building. When over sixty, in 1747, he was invited to Potsdam, near Berlin, where his son Carl Philipp Emanuel worked for the Prussian King Frederick the Great. The King played the flute and knew Bach by repute. When he arrived the King summoned him at once ('Gentlemen, old Bach is here,' he exclaimed) even before Bach had changed his travelling clothes. A concert that was taking place was abandoned and the King led Bach through his palace to try his new pianos—very novel instruments at the time. Frederick gave Bach a theme upon which to improvise a fugue. (Bach later wrote down his improvisation and published it as the first piece in his *Musical Offering*, a set of pieces all based on the King's theme.) This was a crowning occasion in the long career of a performer whose contemporaries called him 'Bach the Great, prince of organists and keyboard players'. The Prussian King gladly recognized an eminence equal to his own, and a power that, while less in the material sense, was to last longer and enlighten the minds and hearts of future generations.

Instruments and Instrumentalists

As we might expect from an age that produced many great performers, the Baroque was also an age of fine instrument makers. The Potsdam pianos were built by the German Silbermann family, more famous for their organs, but the piano was still in its infancy. The main domestic keyboard instrument was still the harpsichord, in which the strings are plucked rather than struck. Some of the best harpsichords had been built rather earlier by the Ruckers family in Antwerp. In Italy, meanwhile, the violin family was developing, and the instruments made by the family firms of Stradivari and Amati have remained unsurpassed. Such fine instruments made possible a school of Italian violinists—Corelli, Geminiani, and above all Antonio Vivaldi (about 1678–1741). One

19

The greatest of violin makers: Antonio Stradivari (1644–1737) in his workshop at Cremona in Italy

contemporary account of Vivaldi's playing said that it had 'not been heard before and can never be equalled ... everyone was astonished'. Another celebrated musician of this time, George Frideric Handel (1685–1759), was a brilliant performer on the harpsichord and organ and on one occasion 'took on' the Italian Domenico Scarlatti in a competition. The result seems to have been that Handel was victorious on the organ and Scarlatti on the harpsichord. Virtuosity was as greatly valued in the eighteenth century as it is today.

The Public Concert and the Orchestra

The performing musician today earns his living by playing in public. But although a paying public attended the theatre in Shakespeare's time, the idea of public concerts came relatively late in musical history; music was supported mainly by the Church or by the aristocracy. The public opera houses of seventeenth-century Venice led the way. Then in London a violinist called John Banister started daily musical performances in 1672. The *London Gazette* of 30 December advertised them as follows: 'At Mr John Banister's house, now called the Musick-school, over against the George Tavern in White Friars, this present Monday, will be musick performed by excellent masters, beginning precisely at four of the

20

clock in the afternoon, and every afternoon for the future, precisely at the same hour.' Admission was one shilling, fairly expensive in those days; but since the Banister concerts continued for six years they were clearly popular.

In 1678 a music-loving coal merchant called Thomas Britton started another concert series that lasted for nearly forty years. A concert hall near Covent Garden market was opened a few years later and enjoyed society patronage, and other series began and apparently flourished. France had her first public concerts in Paris in 1725, and Leipzig, Berlin, Vienna and Stockholm followed. In the 1790s Haydn came to England and presented a group of symphonies at the concerts successfully organized by the violinist and impresario Johann Peter Salomon; these events (from which Haydn made a good deal of money) foreshadowed the 'concert tours' of the nineteenth century. Concert-giving was not confined to major international figures and capital cities. In 1714 the waits of Norwich gave monthly concerts 'for the Accommodation and diversion of the lovers of Musick in this City ... under the summ of One Shilling'.

Thomas Britton of London, a music-loving coal merchant who founded one of the first series of public concerts in 1678

Public interest in music was a strong influence on the growth of the symphony orchestra. Court orchestras were normally quite small, since they normally played to a select audience in a relatively small room. However, when concerts had to be paid for by the public it was necessary to use halls that would accommodate a large audience. To fill such halls with sound more string instruments had to be used—which in turn might mean that the wind department was also enlarged.

There were also musical reasons for the growth of the orchestra, as composers wanted to use a wider range of sounds. Thus in addition to the flutes, oboes, trumpets and horns of Bach's orchestra, clarinets were introduced in the later eighteenth century, just as trombones were to be brought in in the nineteenth by Beethoven in his Fifth Symphony. With these changes the orchestra developed from the small-scale ensemble of the Baroque to the large, dramatic and tonally rich orchestra of Beethoven and the Romantic period.

21

3 Rococo to Romantic

Mozart the Prodigy

In the picturesque Austrian town of Salzburg, Leopold Mozart served as a court musician to Archbishop Sigismund von Schattenbach. There his son Wolfgang Amadeus Mozart was born on 27 January 1756. From the first he was surrounded by music, and he and his sister Nannerl, four years older, were taught to play as soon as they could walk. At four Wolfgang could play little harpsichord pieces, and a year later was making up his own. When he was six he was so advanced that Leopold could not resist the temptation to show him off, and took him to play to the Elector at Munich, then to Vienna and the Imperial court where the Empress Maria Theresa gave the little musician a kiss. He was the star of the occasion, though his very gifted sister performed too. He was given a lilac and gold court dress and Nannerl had one in pink and silver; their father was given a sum of money.

The boy's talents developed rapidly. He learned the violin with the minimum of help from his father. Soon Leopold took his children touring again, this time further afield. At Aix-la-Chapelle in France they played before the sister of Frederick the Great, Princess Amalia of Prussia, and were warmly received. Nevertheless there were practical problems, as Leopold explained in a letter: 'She has no money . . . if the kisses she gave to my children, and Master

Wolfgang in particular, were as many new-coined *louis d'or*, we should be fortunate enough. But neither my landlord at the inn, nor the postmaster, are to be contented with kisses.' In Brussels Leopold hoped to perform for Prince Charles of Lorraine, but they were obliged to wait upon this nobleman's pleasure—'his highness the prince does nothing but hunt, gobble and swill, and we may in the end discover that he has no money ... what with snuff-boxes, leather cases and such-like pretty playthings we shall soon be able to open a shop'.

Leopold Mozart was a sharply practical man, but he lacked the imagination to realize that not many wealthy people in his time were patrons and con-noisseurs of the arts. Music was for them just a pleasant diversion, like sport or cards. At the French court of Versailles in 1764 the Mozarts attended a royal dinner party. The children stood with the servants near the table and the queen passed Wolfgang a few tasty morsels, as if he were a pet dog. That was the kind of world Mozart lived in. Still, when the family went on to London to play for King George III they received a friendly and un-ceremonious welcome. Wolfgang played for the queen, who sang, and he also performed on the organ and improvised on a Handel aria. 'Only twenty-four guineas' was Leopold's account of their reward; but the young musician's meeting with J. S. Bach's son Johann Christian was of lasting value, for this 'London' Bach taught him much. Mozart was in-credibly precocious, and composed symphonies

The boy Mozart at the Austrian Court in 1762: the Archduke Joseph is presenting him to the Empress Maria Theresa

Mozart in his thirties:
an anonymous
engraving made after
his death

before reaching the age of ten.

When he grew up, Mozart had to earn his living. When he was seventeen his father tried to get him a post at the Imperial court in Vienna, but nothing came of the idea. In the meantime he was employed by the new archbishop, who seems to have tolerated his frequent absences for music-making in Italy, Germany or France; but the atmosphere then changed and he was made to feel less comfortable. Finally he was forcibly ejected from the archbishop's presence after a stormy interview. 'I hate the archbishop almost to fury', he told his anxious father. He left Salzburg in 1781 for the Austrian capital Vienna.

In Vienna Mozart earned a living by giving concerts of his music—especially piano concertos in which he directed the orchestra from the keyboard as was then the fashion—and also by teaching. He was paid for composing (a new opera, for example), and he might make some money from the sale of printed compositions. But he described himself as 'without a penny of secure income' and towards the end of his life was obliged to beg for money from friends. He became ill, partly with overwork and worry, and died at the tragically early age of thirty-five. Mozart's letters give us a vivid picture of his life and times. One written from a monastery in Germany in 1777 tells us of his skill and showmanship as a keyboard player:

> Everyone praised my beautiful, pure tone. Afterwards they brought in a small clavichord and I improvised and then played a sonata and the Fischer variations. Then the others whispered to the dean that he should just hear me play something in the organ style. I asked him to give me a theme. He declined, but one of the monks gave me one. I put it through its paces and played something quite lively, though in the same tempo; and after that the theme over again, but this time backside first. Finally it occurred to me, could I not use my lively tune as the theme for a fugue?

A Freelance Performer: Beethoven

Where Mozart had failed, in that despite his widely recognised gifts he died in poverty, Ludwig van

24

Ludwig van Beethoven

Beethoven succeeded. Beethoven was born in 1770, just fourteen years after Mozart, at Bonn in Germany; though he too later made his home in Vienna. Like Mozart's, his childhood was musical, but it was less happy, not least because of his father's heavy drinking and the way that he selfishly exploited his son's obvious talents for his own profit. But the young Beethoven made good friends, both among local musicians and the friendly nobility, with whom he made relationships of real equality. He had a job as a viola player in the Electoral orchestra at Bonn, but at twenty-one set off for Vienna. In theory, he was on leave and still received his salary, but wartime events stopped the payments after about eighteen months.

However, by that time Beethoven had made influential friends in Vienna and enjoyed free lodging at the house of Prince Lichnowsky. As a brilliant young pianist he soon gathered around him

25

well-to-do pupils from high society; by dedicating his works to princes or an archduke he earned financial reward as well as prestige; sometimes his wealthy friends would subscribe to the publication of his music; finally, he could perform at fashionable *soirées* for a fee.

Beethoven was well known as a pianist in his own day, whose vivid imagination and expressive powers were unequalled. In particular he developed a smooth, 'singing' style that was to be so typical of the Romantic pianists. This was made possible by the development of the piano, which in Mozart's day had been a small, lightly-built instrument that was not capable of 'big' tone. Like Mozart and Bach before him, Beethoven was a fine improviser, as his pupil Carl Czerny recalled:

His improvisation was brilliant and striking—in whatever company he might chance to be he knew how to achieve such an effect upon every listener, that frequently not an eye remained dry, while many would break out into loud sobs, for there was something wonderful in his expression in addition to the beauty and originality of his ideas and the spirited style of rendering them.

Beethoven was also a conductor, and directed performances of his symphonies and other orchestral works, and seems to have anticipated the modern 'acrobatic' school of conducting. A contemporary wrote that 'when, in his opinion, a passage was to be played *piano*, he would creep almost under the music-stand, and when he wanted *forte* he would leap upwards with the most curious gestures and utter the strangest sounds.' But this was in his later career, when he was tragically handicapped by deafness. The orchestra would quietly ignore his conducting and follow a beat given by the first violinist; for Beethoven, it seems, could not even hear the audience's applause. At the piano, too, he would sometimes play so lightly that the instrument would produce no sound at all: 'He hears it himself in the "mind's ear"', it was said. But of course the ending of his performer's career did not mean the end of his musical life, for he remained one of the greatest of composers.

One great artist paints
another: Chopin by
Eugène Delacroix,
foremost of French
Romantic painters

The Age of the Virtuoso

The nineteenth century is the time of the Romantic
composers; and for them the piano became an ideal
instrument. Some of the short pieces by Schubert,
Schumann or Mendelssohn belong in the home
rather than the concert hall, for they are gentle,
domestic music. On the other hand a ballade by
Chopin or a Hungarian rhapsody by Liszt have a
grandeur and fire that suit a concert grand piano and
a correspondingly large auditorium. Chopin was
Polish by birth, and Liszt Hungarian. But both these
men (born in 1810 and 1811 respectively) spent much
of their working life in Paris, for each was a brilliant
pianist and Paris was in the 1830s a great pianistic
center. Not all the pianists who toured to Paris or
settled there were French. There was the Irishman
John Field, whose fingers, it was said, 'poured over
the keys as pearls on velvet' and whose playing was
'exquisitely spiritual, coupled with surprising ap-
lomb and coquetry'. The Bohemian Jan Ladislav
Dussek's fingers drew from the piano 'delicious yet
emphatic tones, like a company of ten singers
endowed with equal skill'. The German Kalkbrenner
played with 'a clearness, a distinctness and a
neatness that are astonishing'. These pianists played

to audiences who paid for the privilege; the piano recital was born in this early Romantic period. The word 'recital' was actually first used by Liszt in 1840.

Chopin played with finesse rather than sheer power. Mendelssohn thought him 'entirely original, a perfect virtuoso'. He himself explained that, as a pianist, he had a 'perhaps overbold but not ignoble desire to create a new world', and his sensitive style made many of his contemporaries seem crude by comparison. A few complained that he played too softly, and his playing was doubtless more suited to a salon than a large hall. In any case, despite his success as a pianist, he disliked playing in public ('he fears the public', said his friend George Sand) and performed infrequently. The very rarity of his appearances enhanced his fame.

The most celebrated Romantic pianist, however, was Franz Liszt. Liszt toured all over Europe, and even to Turkey, earning vast sums and attracting

A caricature of the pianist Franz Liszt, showing him as the 'aged darling' of beautiful and fashionable ladies

large and occasionally hysterical audiences. In 1831, at the age of nineteen, he had heard the legendary violinist Paganini and determined to become a pianist of the same fantastic order of mastery and brilliance. He practised for up to twelve hours daily, and wrote, 'if I don't go mad, you'll find in me the sort of artist we need today'. He composed, for himself, the twelve 'transcendental studies' that were considered so difficult as to be 'for most ten or twelve players in the world'. His career was extraordinarily successful, the main problem being the ladies who found his magnetism irresistible and who pursued him even when he was touring. (One suspects that his travels may occasionally have been designed to shake them off!) He had three children, one of whom, Cosima, eventually married the composer Richard Wagner. Another lady—a princess, in fact— finally persuaded him, while still only thirty-five, to give up the performer's life and settle down to compose music instead. But even in his later years he retained his performing genius. At the age of seventy-four he played in Rome for the young Frenchman Claude Debussy, who remembered his use of the piano's sustaining pedal as 'a kind of breathing'.

Masters of the Violin

The Italian violin makers and performers of the Baroque had their most illustrious successor in the legendary Niccolò Paganini (1782–1840). He was born in Genoa, and his father was a music-lover who gave the boy his first violin lessons. His mother used to tell him of her dream in which an angel promised her that her son would become the greatest violinist in the world. Ironically, his apparently superhuman powers when he reached maturity inspired rumours that he had sold his soul to the devil in exchange for his genius! A great showman, Paganini did not deny the story. He used to dress in black, a tall figure who glided on to the stage wearing dark blue glasses; and with his pale complexion the impression was 'of a bleached skull with a violin locked under its chin'. Paganini's skill, and his playing style too, were unique; he was the supreme virtuoso. And his fees were accordingly high: invited to England to play at the time of William IV's coronation, he received a fee

Paganini: a
daguerreotype taken
shortly before his death
in 1840. His left-hand
stretch was evidently
exceptional

of a thousand guineas, worth about £40,000 or
$95,000 in today's terms. There were a few—perhaps
those who had not heard him—who thought that no
one could possibly be worth that kind of money. In
England there was a rhyme about Paganini:

Who are those who pay five guineas,
To hear this tune of Paganini's?
Echo answers—'Pack o' ninnies'.

But it seems that all who actually heard him play—as brilliantly upon a single string as on all four—were won over and never forgot the experience. The music he wrote for his instrument is still considered the most difficult that exists.

Joseph Joachim and Fritz Kreisler, the former born in 1831 and the latter in 1875, were violinists of a different kind. Neither possessed the particular kind of technique and dazzling showmanship of Paganini. On the other hand, they brought to violin playing great qualities of insight and imagination. It was for Joachim that Brahms composed his Violin Concerto in 1878. Kreisler, who also came from the German-speaking part of Europe, made his public debut at seven, as Joachim had done; by the age of fifteen he had finished his studies and had even toured America. Then, mysteriously, he gave up music for several years and became an army officer. Coming back to the violin, he played a few times in public without much success. But then, with great effort, he recovered his skills and from 1899 pursued a brilliant career in Europe and America.

Kreisler is not the only performer who has felt the need to withdraw from public performance for a while after a dazzling start. In our own time Yehudi Menuhin similarly had a period of reflection after early fame as a prodigy, and so did the pianist Maurizio Pollini, who explained a four-year silence simply by saying, 'I wanted to become a better musician'. Perhaps Kreisler's situation was similar. Certainly in his maturity he was admired above all as a 'poet' of the violin rather than a technical wizard. Sir Edward Elgar's deeply personal Violin Concerto of 1910 was dedicated to Kreisler and first performed by him. Kreisler seems to belong to the twentieth century, more perhaps than Paganini would have done. Audiences today take technical mastery for granted and look especially for qualities of individuality and imagination, expecting a performer to reveal new beauties even in familiar music.

4 Andrew Lloyd Webber The Composer's View

At only thirty-two Andrew Lloyd Webber is recognised as being an outstanding composer with a list of major successes to his name. What is more, he has gained his reputation with popular stage musicals—a form that has in recent years proved hazardous financially.

With lyricist Tim Rice he has written *Joseph and the Amazing Technicolor Dreamcoat, Jesus Christ Superstar* and, of course, *Evita*. He collaborated with playwright Alan Ayckbourn on the doomed production *Jeeves*, and with Don Black on the highly praised concert piece *Tell Me On A Sunday*.

He has also composed an instrumental work called *Variations* for his brother, cellist Julian Lloyd Webber, and is currently involved in staging his new musical *Cats*, in which he has set to music a collection of poems by T. S. Eliot.

The fact that Andrew Lloyd Webber has achieved so much by such a young age may in part stem from his background. He was born into a musical family—in fact his father is at present director of the London College of Music and was director of the composition department at the Royal College of Music. Andrew was therefore given every opportunity from an early age to learn an instrument or, to be more precise, three—violin, piano and French horn.

'I think my mother was very keen that we should all learn as many instruments as possible in the hope

Andrew Lloyd Webber
during rehearsal for his
opera *Evita*

that one of them would stick. I was more interested in
the French horn really, but the piano was the thing I
played for myself all the time because I found I could
compose on that,' he explains.

His interest in musicals was stimulated by his
aunt—herself an actress—who took him as a child to
see lots of different shows. And by the time he was
about eight Andrew knew he wanted to compose
rather than perform himself.

'I built myself a small theatre to play with and in
fact I had my first music published then because my
father collated some of the bits and pieces I was

33

writing for musicals and got them published in a magazine. Unfortunately,' he smiles, 'I've lost it, and I've always wanted to know what the tunes were in case they were useful!'

His parents were quite strict about practising, and Andrew as well as his brother Julian attended the Royal College of Music junior department on Saturday mornings. This continued until he went to Westminster public school which ran classes on Saturdays. From then on academic work distracted Andrew from his music, although he still managed to write a couple of musicals—with lyrics by one of the prefects—in his first two years there.

'I was developing a sort of technique. I was forming my tunes and themes and I loved doing it. I was becoming very interested in the actual mathematics of melody.'

He says he was very much influenced by great popular composers like Richard Rodgers and George Gershwin: 'I really didn't start to develop what I would call an absolutely defined language of my own until I was about fifteen or sixteen.'

However not only was Andrew a prodigious young composer, he was also extremely interested in history and architecture and when only seventeen he won an exhibition to Magdalen College, Oxford, to study history.

Nevertheless, because he had made up his mind that his future lay with the musical theatre ('There was absolutely no question of doing anything else') Andrew subsequently went to the Guildhall School of Music and finally the Royal College to catch up on his musical training. At the time his father was not entirely happy about this.

'He felt that my kind of rather natural writing for melody would actually get educated out of me by formal courses.'

Although Andrew now agrees that there was some danger of this happening, he does not underestimate the value of attending a music college.

'It's very important to get a grounding in what certain musical instruments can do, as well as in composition, harmony and orchestration.'

He says that in his time he was only taught conventional orchestration, but it is completely

34

different these days.

'Many of the modern, contemporary "serious musicians" now cross right over and understand the value of pop, rock and musical because there's so little of value happening in contemporary serious music. When I was at college the idea of somebody like Julian playing *Variations* would just have been met with horror!'

Tim Rice and Andrew Lloyd Webber originally met in 1964 through some mutual friends who knew Andrew was looking for a lyricist.

The first real interest in their work arose when they wrote a musical about Dr Barnardo, a nineteenth-century philanthropist. It was going to be staged in Oxford when a West End producer offered to put it on in London instead. But ultimately, as so often is the case, the promised London production never happened.

'So lesson number one in music is it's much the most important thing to get your work on *somewhere* and not have the thing buried. If it had only been done at Oxford it would have given us a marvellous chance to see exactly what the strengths and weaknesses of the piece were.'

In 1968 they were asked to write something for schoolchildren to perform at an end-of-term concert, so the Lloyd Webber/Rice partnership finally made its public debut 'on a Friday afternoon to a load of indifferent parents!'

The production, *Joseph and the Amazing Technicolor Dreamcoat*, got such a good reception in spite of its modest venue, that it was published by the music publishers Novello's and performed again at the Central Hall, Westminster, where Andrew's father was organist.

'We had the whole place full that time,' he remembers, 'and we got a rave review in *The Sunday Times*. This was what really started us off because it was that review that got a record company to call us and say, "We'd like to have this piece."'

In fact it was not until the early '70s and with a much extended version of the show that *Joseph* was produced in the West End. But in the meantime it indirectly led to Tim Rice and Andrew Lloyd Webber's first huge success.

Andrew Lloyd Webber
with his collaborator,
the lyricist Tim Rice

'We did a performance of *Joseph* in St Paul's
Cathdral just before the record came out in 1969, and
the dean of the Cathedral—an excellent man called
Martin Sullivan, who has just recently died— said,
"Why don't you do the story of Christ?" We were a
little nervous about the idea and we thought it would
be more interesting if it was seen through the eyes of
Judas Iscariot.'

This, of course, was how *Jesus Christ Superstar*
came to be written.

The combination of Andrew and Tim created the
right chemistry to produce a totally fresh approach
to musicals. Andrew has strong views on this subject,

'I'm convinced that people are fed up and bored to
tears with conventional musical subjects. Once in a
while you get a conventional musical that proves me
wrong, like *Annie*; but on the whole I think people
want an experience in the theatre that's quite
different now.'

Jesus Christ Superstar came out on record long
before it was produced on stage, and the album found
a market in America 'when we couldn't give copies
away in England! *Superstar* came out in America at a
time when everyone was talking about young people
turning back to religion and there'd been various
sorts of cults like Jesus freaks. And in the middle
of all this came *Jesus Christ Superstar*, which
with hindsight everybody thinks was carefully
orchestrated—but of course it wasn't.

36

The record's success meant that they were able to do *Superstar* on stage, although Tim and Andrew had to rework a lot of it because it could not be performed in exactly the way it had been produced on disc. And it wasn't until the Broadway opening that there was any mention of it at all in the British papers, despite the fact that Andrew and Tim had already made the cover of *Time* magazine in the States.

'You know we were just enormous in America. But that sort of spectacular reaction is not always very good because it means that you're going to find it very hard next time around. In my view we were still paying the price of that over-exaggerated [*Superstar*] launch when the *Evita* reviews appeared, even though *Evita* has now gone so well in America,'

Although his music was first widely appreciated in America, he still thinks that the British are more receptive to new ideas.

'You've got more chance with an original musical in Britain than you have in America really, and things like *Tell Me On A Sunday* or *Variations* aren't really successful in America.'

Jesus Christ Superstar ran in the West End for an

Andrew with Hal Prince, producer of *Evita*, and Elaine Page who sang the title role in the London production

astounding eight years before it closed. Tim and Andrew, of course went on to write *Evita*, based on an idea of Tim's, and this too has been hugely successful on both sides of the Atlantic. But not all Andrew's projects have been triumphs, and he is perfectly frank about the reasons why *Jeeves* failed.

'There was no unity between the script and the music; it was overlong and just not very good. It should have been taken off when it was out of London, put into mothballs and reworked.'

Obviously the marriage of words and music has to be just right and normally when working with Tim, Andrew writes the tunes first and then the words are added. With Don Black on *Tell Me On A Sunday* it was about half and half, but with *Cats* Andrew has had to fit the music to the lyrics because they consist of already existing poems by T.S. Eliot.

'Melodies are very much about rhythm, and the rhythm as much as anything else will give you the musicality. If you take a chorus like "OH! Well I never!/ Was there ever/ A Cat so clever/ As Magical Mr Mistoffelees!" from Eliot's words, there are certain shapes that it has to take, so the tune *must* go in a certain way—which is something you discover.

'I'm quite pleased that I have done it this way round because for a long time I thought I wouldn't be able to. Though of course, I am working with very fine verse.'

When writing musicals the composer also has to consider what's happening to the storyline in a particular scene.

'If I'm not actually listening to the rhythm of the words I'm setting, then I'm thinking of the visual images that are naturally conjured up.'

Film scores demand less in many ways from the composer because he's simply shown the finished film and, as Andrew says, 'just puts on it what "they" want.' For this reason he isn't particulary keen to do another movie—he wrote the scores for *Gumshoe* and *The Odessa File*—but he does admit that the reason he hasn't found the experience musically challenging may partly be because he hasn't had a good enough relationship with the directors concerned.

'If I were going to do something for the cinema now,

I would like it to be an original piece written for the cinema where the music has an identity in its own right. It does in certain films like *Close Encounters*, which is an example of how music has been very well and very intelligently used. But the majority of feature films offer nothing for the composer.'

Musicals, on the other hand, have given Andrew enormous creative scope not only to work on the music but to shape the whole production. When collaborating with Tim Rice, he always has a fairly clear idea of how their musical would be staged even if, initially, only an album were released.

'Quite a lot of people forget that many of the production ideas that there are in the stage version of *Evita*—magnificently directed as it is—were actually in the original white album sleeve notes,' Andrew observes.

In fact it was so well thought out in advance that they had to alter very little in *Evita* in order to stage it, but he admits that *Superstar* should have had many more changes made to it.

'But, you see, we couldn't because it was so well known by the time we came to put on the show that it was just impossible to alter. We had to do a tremendous amount to the orchestration and production of *Superstar* to try and overcome the fact that we were saddled with a record.'

Andrew composes on the piano and says he just writes when he feels like it. He generally performs his new pieces at the festival he holds in the country every year from which he produces a tape recording that he can work on further, listening to it over and over again.

When composing a musical Andrew claims that the most important element of all is the contruction, although naturally the melodies must also be good and the words literate and intelligent.

'You can literally manipulate an audience by the construction, I think you could take one of the greatest melodies that Richard Rodgers ever wrote like 'Some Enchanted Evening' and say that if it had been in the wrong place in the wrong musical it would have been completely buried. Nobody was more aware of the craft of how to put together a musical—just from the point of view of getting his

The 1973 film of the Webber-Rice *Jesus Christ Superstar* was made partly in Israel. Some of the most imaginative music came in the crucifixion scene

tunes heard—than Richard Rodgers.'

The construction is even more important to the composer when, unlike the typical musical that has a lot of spoken dialogue and a few songs, the music runs all the way through it—*Evita* is 140 minutes of music! Through such shows Andrew has learned that audiences can only absorb a certain number of original melodies in an evening.

'I've often found when I've bombarded people with things and tried to do things that are a little more harmonically unusual, people tend to come back and say, "Well, there's only one or two tunes in it," because they simply cannot receive beyond a certain amount.'

He thinks that structure is equally important in instrumental pieces. '*Variations* is a very simple form for people to understand—it's just a theme with variations. And I know that one of the reasons that it is a success is that people have got a very defined structure that they can latch on to.'

Interestingly, although *Variations* has been Andrew's biggest selling record in Britain, he insists that he would still be very concerned if he were asked to write a concerto for Julian.

'But I know that if I were to go that way I would very much follow the Prokofiev mould and base it pretty heavily on classical principles because it seems to me that the majority of great pieces are very strongly influenced by form.'

Orchestration, Andrew confesses, is for him the slogging, boring part of composition: getting it down on paper. Actually he is so busy these days that he has been working with one or two other people who co-orchestrate with him, but he's not entirely happy with the arrangement because he says he inevitably starts fiddling about with things at the band rehearsal stage. Yet it must be remembered that conventional orchestration has rather gone out the window since modern electronic instruments became available.

'With *Variations*— which finally came down to being a precisely written score—I had an overall idea that a certain type of synthesizer could do a certain thing, but I didn't know exactly what it was. I had an idea of the colour of the piece but the sheer range of what these things are able to do now is something you keep discovering all the time. In the course of making a record you find other new sounds.'

He intends to make full use of electronic instruments in the forthcoming production of *Cats*. A quarter of the orchestra will be electronic and at least three synthesizers will be playing at once.

Composition is inevitably a lot of hard work as well as inspiration and Andrew reckons that he throws out a lot of material on the way—for example, a good two-thirds of *Tell Me On A Sunday* was rewritten many times. But the satisfactions of being a composer are immense, although Andrew confesses that it's very difficult to say which of his own compositions

41

give him the greatest pleasure.

'I think probably as a total work *Variations* is my best piece. It is essentially very frothy—a celebration of technique—and all the musicians involved have to be able to play incredibly well. From that point of view the theatricality of the thing is like watching a well organized firework display.'

Also, when in the last third of *Evita* he explores subjects like melancholy and death, he was extremely pleased to find that the audience accepted them very easily.

'It was a great thrill for me at the first preview of *Evita* in London during the long scene where we have Eva and Peron arguing in two adjacent bedrooms, that it actually got a round of applause.'

However he says that nothing quite compares with the thrill you get when you first hear your music played by an orchestra—an experience that can't be repeated.

'I now have a very good idea of what anything I write down on paper is going to sound like. So the most exciting moment that you have is when you're just beginning and you've never had access to an orchestra before.'

In Andrew's opinion the most important thing for any young composers to do is to get their music heard and played. Firstly, like *Joseph*, if it's any good it will be picked up: and secondly, it's the only way to actually hear your work and consequently learn from it. He points out that the latter is much easier these days.

'Tape recorders are so much cheaper and better and synthesizers are relatively cheap, so you can do quite complicated things at home which a few years ago would have cost you a fortune in equipment. As a result I think any younger composer must take a very serious stock of the new synthesizers and things that are around and improving all the time.'

He is very encouraging about the chances of good work being appreciated. 'People in the music industry are in fact crying out the whole time for new, talented people. It's just unfortunate that a lot of people—myself included—don't always recognise when the work they're doing isn't quite good enough. Hence *Jeeves*,' he states wryly.

Andrew thinks his own lasting reputation depends on what he writes in the next ten years, although he hopes if *Cats* is a success it may make people take his previous work more seriously.

'If all I wrote was what I have written up till now, certain pieces would continue to be performed but people wouldn't say that I was on the level of the Rodgers and Sondheims because I don't think I'm quite at the age when they started writing at their very best. It's also a question of time. You don't really get recognized or established until you've done a very large body of work.'

Whether or not his music lives on is less important to Andrew than the fact that he enjoys composing at the time, and he still has many things he wants to explore musically.

'I would like to investigate certain subjects and things within music that I don't think I'd have dared to touch before. But I have two sides to me really because at the same time I don't ever want to be so obscure in my writing that people don't understand what I'm doing.'

He believes that contemporary serious music has fallen into this trap and has become too elitist for people to relate to. And he can't see it advancing very much until it retrenches and takes another direction.

He fervently hopes that his own great love—the musical theatre—will continue to develop with innovative shows as it has done in the past with *West Side Story*, and more currently with *Evita* and *Sweeney Todd*. And there is every chance if Andrew Lloyd Webber keeps writing musicals that he, more than anyone else, will advance his own cause and create 'a public that will be more prepared to get excited when they are given a large theatre experience.'

5 The Conductor

The Conductor's Role

From the *aulos* player Sakados in the sixth century B.C. to the pianist Pollini, born in 1942, we have so far looked at individual performers or soloists. It is their own personality that makes their art 'creative'. The individual player presents the music in his own way. Of course, he must be faithful to what the composer wrote. The Chilean pianist Claudio Arrau has said that this faithfulness is the essential base of an interpretation but cannot be the whole story. 'It is the springboard from which an interpreter can take off ... the firmer the base the greater can be the flights of true musical imagination.' Arrau particularly admired the conductor Wilhelm Furtwängler performing a Beethoven symphony—'he had the power of divination'.

Thus in a way, the conductor too is a solo performer. It is his interpretation, and no one else's, that the orchestra gives us. Paradoxically, the conductor's art is 'silent': his name may appear in larger letters than the composer's on a record sleeve, but he makes none of the sounds that emerge from your loudspeaker! It is also ironic that he was only needed because of the rise of *ensemble* music (music for groups of performers). As the orchestra developed during the seventeenth and eighteenth centuries it became necessary for someone to 'lead' the players, who had to be kept together in the performance of an overture, a symphony—or an opera, with the singers on stage and the orchestra below them. Indeed the basic matter of speeds needed one person in control— hence the conductor's most obvious task, that of beating time with his 'baton' (a light stick).

But there is of course far more to conducting than beating time. In anything other than the shortest and simplest piece of music, speed (or 'tempo') will vary, not only from one section to the next but also in speeding up (*accelerando*) and slowing down (*rallentando*). The texture and balance of the music are also the conductor's responsibility, for only he can hear if, say, the string accompaniment to a flute solo is at the right level of loudness. It is he who must decide what kind of 'tone colour' is to be heard: whether the strings should sound more mysterious, or more

Sir Thomas Beecham (1879–1961), a *grand seigneur* among English conductors who excelled in Mozart and Delius. His last concert was as late as 1960 on the 7th May, at the Guildhall, Portsmouth

45

expressively vibrant, or whether the 'attack' of the trumpets has enough sharpness and bite. He must also judge whether the orchestra is strictly 'in tune', in other words ensuring that no instruments are sharp or flat, and being able to identify whose instrument may be 'off the note' without fuss or time-wasting. In some ways the conductor is like the director of a play, or the manager of a football team, for he directs the rehearsals or practice games. But there is a difference, because he also directs the performance itself and can instantly modify the playing if need be. The orchestra must therefore attend to his every gesture. Indeed, the conductor almost 'plays the orchestra' as a pianist plays the piano; the individual players in an orchestra, however skilled as individuals, are here merely part of one great 'instrument'.

The conductor directs a performance by his gestures, and even facial expressions. In the earliest days, his baton might have been a real stick, and indeed the composer Lully died in Paris in 1687 after striking his foot with the heavy stick that he used to beat time on the floor. A less crude alternative was to tap a music-desk. One of Bach's predecessors in Leipzig liked to wave a roll of music paper at his singers and instrumentalists. When Mozart or Beethoven played a piano concerto with an orchestra, they directed from the keyboard often without actually beating time at all.

At Oxford in the late eighteenth century, Haydn conducted a symphony from the organ. Where no keyboard instrument was playing, the first violinist might gesture with his bow, and when Mendelssohn used a baton to conduct the first London performance of his oratorio *Elijah* in 1847, the first violinist was determined also to exercise his usual role and insisted on 'conducting' as well, while a music critic complained that Mendelssohn had obstructed the view of the 'real' conductor as well as confusing the players! The baton took a good while to be accepted. As a matter of fact, even today some conductors prefer to direct the music just with their hands. Leopold Stokowski, the legendary conductor of the Philadelphia Orchestra, was one of these; and Pierre Boulez is another.

Qualifications of a Conductor

Above all, a conductor must lead the orchestra, for the players will not play as he wishes unless they respect his musicianship and baton technique. But of course, he must give and take. Say, for example, that a trumpet player cannot play a high passage as softly as desirable: it may be sensible for the conductor to accept slightly louder playing without fuss. He often asks the advice of the leading first violinist about string bowing (in which all the players must agree), or consults a woodwind soloist about phrasing—that is, the 'shaping' of the music in terms of breathing, tonguing, volume of tone and that rhythmic freedom which is called *rubato*. He has to decide how much time to spend on each piece during rehearsal—and because of the high cost of an orchestra's time, good judgement here is essential.

The famous first conductor of the Promenade Concerts in London, Sir Henry Wood, once listed the following essentials for the would-be conductor:

1. A complete general knowledge of music.
2. A more than slight acquaintance with every instrument of the orchestra, and if possible some intensive study of a string instrument— preferably the violin.
3. Ability to play the piano well.

Two English conductors, Sir Henry Wood (left) and Sir Adrian Boult, preparing for the 1942 season of Promenade Concerts in London

47

4. An impeccably sensitive ear, as well as a rhythmic and interpretative sense.
5. Confidence in the art of gesture.
6. Perfect sight-reading ability and sound musicianship.
7. Knowledge of the art of singing.
8. A good physique, a good temper, and a strong sense of discipline.

These points are as valid today as they were when Sir Henry's book was published in 1945. Of course the conductor must be familiar with a wide repertory of orchestral music, and with the various instruments that play under his direction. The acquaintance with the instruments goes further than knowing what notes they can play: ideally he will know his own players' strong and weak points and shape his performance accordingly. As for the violin family, the strings are the largest orchestral section and the foundation of the orchestral sound. The piano-playing skill is for work done behind the scenes, like preliminary rehearsal with a concerto soloist or a singer, so that points of interpretation can be decided before rehearsal with the orchestra. With a new or unfamiliar work, too, the conductor needs to get to know the music before going into rehearsal. The 'sensitive ear' covers that tricky matter of playing in tune. This is not something which can be taken for granted even with skilled orchestral musicians, for it is a question of the relative pitch between one instrument and another. It is the conductor, too, who must adjust, if necessary, to the particular acoustics of a hall (the effect of the building on the sound). If it is especially 'resonant' (producing echoes), for example, he may ask the orchestra for a 'drier' sound (shorter notes) than normal to compensate. The conductor can listen better than any individual orchestral player, and must, for the overall sound quality is entirely his responsibility. His gestures must be purposeful and clear to communicate to the players. The right hand gives the beat, while the left is more concerned with expression. But the conductor need not dance about on the rostrum, as Igor Stravinsky rather mischievously made clear when he called Leonard Bernstein 'an impressive jumper ... he could get a dozen curtain calls out of the

Riccardo Muti, born in
Naples in 1941, is
already an established
conductor on the
international scene, in
both the concert hall
and the opera house

National Anthem'.

Sight-reading skill is needed because a conductor's
music—the full orchestral score itself—is far more
complex than that of an individual player. Indeed he
must scan the music of every orchestral instrument
simultaneously. As for singing, he will accompany a
singer or direct a chorus better if he knows about
breathing. It is also he who must, for example, choose
the four solo singers for Beethoven's Ninth Symphony and ensure a well-balanced and blended group
of voices. His choice of singers for Handel's *Messiah*
will differ from his selection for Verdi's *Requiem*,
because different music may demand other vocal or
interpretative qualities. His own singing voice can
be important for identifying a phrase in rehearsal and
perhaps even showing how it should be 'shaped'; and
a clear speaking voice too is essential if the orchestra
is to understand his instructions.

49

Opposite: Igor
Stravinsky conducts the
USSR Symphony
Orchestra in Moscow,
in September 1962. It
was his first visit to his
native Russia for over
forty years

Physical and mental well-being go inevitably with a job in which the conductor is more continuously active than most, if not all, of his players. Many conductors, amazingly, have carried their careers on into their eighties—Beecham, Boult, Toscanini, Stokowski, and Klemperer, to name a few. Self-discipline means that the conductor must attend rehearsal punctually and well-prepared, and according to Sir Henry Wood, 'be friendly, but not "pally"', so that the players' response, both personally and in terms of performance quality, will be as great as possible.

Training a Conductor

Of course Sir Henry Wood's requirements of a conductor are all desirable. But the fact remains that eight-year-old infant prodigies like the Italian Pierino Gamba (today a mature conductor) have conducted quite acceptable performances. An orchestra can, at least up to a point, perform familiar music simply by following its lead violinist just as happens in a string quartet. Indeed in 1922 the Persimfans Orchestra of Moscow was proud to be democratically conductorless, and the same experiment has been tried in New York. Today, however, neither of these cities has such an orchestra, which suggests that the conductor does indeed have a vital role.

Many conductors, strangely enough, have had little or no formal training. Some have been orchestral players who later took up the baton: thus Serge Koussevitzky was a double bass virtuoso, Sir John Barbirolli a cellist, Pierre Monteux a viola player and Sir Colin Davis a clarinettist. The French conductor Pierre Boulez has said he just 'fell into' conducting: 'I quickly discovered that I was able to conduct without taking any lessons: I think one can learn to conduct only by conducting.' Recently several pianists have taken up the baton, including Daniel Barenboim and Vladimir Ashkenazy. The cellist Mstislav Rostropovich holds a conductorship in Washington. Even the singer Dietrich Fischer-Dieskau has conducted Berlioz, Brahms and Schubert. Composers are often asked to conduct performances of their own music, and these too seem to manage without any special training—Stravinsky

and Britten are examples. When Stravinsky conducted his ballet *The Rite of Spring* for a recording in
1928, he was, he says, 'nervous about doing it at first,
in view of its reputation as a difficult piece, but these
famous difficulties ... proved to be a conductor's
myth; *The Rite* is arduous but not difficult'. Not for
Stravinsky, perhaps; but he has been very critical of
performances of this work by other conductors!

In 1978 *The Rite of Spring* was recorded by a very young English conductor, Simon Rattle, with the National Youth Orchestra—which says much for present standards in English music. Simon Rattle's training is perhaps more typical than that of the artists mentioned above: for him conducting was a major aim early in his career. Born in Liverpool in 1955, he played as a percussionist and then went to the Royal Academy of Music in London where his main subjects were conducting and the piano. In 1974 he won an international conducting competition and was later appointed Assistant Conductor of the Bournemouth Symphony Orchestra. Since then he has become established with regular BBC work and a good deal of freelance activity, all before reaching the age of twenty-five. Simon Rattle is now strongly placed to join the ranks of the well-paid and jet-setting conductors of the international circuit whose present leaders are such men as Karajan, Solti, Haitink and Bernstein—artists whose reputation is worldwide and who are paid around £4,000 ($9,500) for a single appearance. Nevertheless he faces stiff competition. Every year there is a fresh crop of 'brilliant young conductors' whom the record companies have signed up to make new recordings of the standard orchestral repertory. Despite the bally-hoo, not all will survive.

One of today's most distinguished conductors, Herbert von Karajan, who has made his Berlin Philharmonic Orchestra into one of the finest in the world

Postscript

'What is Pyramus?' asks Bottom in Shakespeare's *A Midsummer Night's Dream*, 'a lover, or a tyrant?' Orchestral musicians might ask the same about a conductor. 'Conductors are too often rude and conceited tyrants', said the composer Shostakovich: 'in my youth I often had to fight fierce battles with them'. Arturo Toscanini was this Russian composer's pet hate. On the other hand the British orchestral viola player Bernard Shore spoke more positively of the celebrated Italian maestro: 'Personal magnetism . . . radiates from the man and holds each of us, not in a grip of iron, but with a power at once irresistible and intensely human and sympathetic. Toscanini is aloof . . . but he is no superman; he is a truly human being.' However, Bernard Shore also admired Sir Adrian Boult for not having 'the prima donna's temperament usually found in famous conductors' and added that this quiet Englishman, very different from the fiery Toscanini, was surpassed by few in the art of true interpretation.

And how do the conductors see themselves? As something of a 'traffic cop', says André Previn, for whom the satisfying thing is 'to make great music with a great orchestra'. Neville Marriner admits that 'everyone likes to be boss' and values the feeling of fulfilment associated with a conductor's complete responsibility for a performance. Sir David Willcocks has modestly but eloquently said: 'why I enjoy conducting is that one is making music with people and sharing the emotions, the feelings of joy, which result from that activity.' Pierre Boulez, whose aim may sometimes seem sheer precision and control, once confessed that conducting 'intoxicated' him. The truth is that conductors differ in personality as much as composers. This is fortunate, for it avoids monotony, and between them they can cover the immense repertory of orchestral music; thus, for example, we do not find the repertory of Sir Thomas Beecham—Mozart, Sibelius, Delius—in the concerts directed by Pierre Boulez, who specializes in more challenging new music. There is room in the concert hall for all tastes. And orchestral musicians today seem to be able to play anything!

6 The String Players

The Violin Family

The violin has been called the most unnatural way of making music that exists—by a professional violinist! An instrument weighing about a pound has to be held up on the left shoulder, while the right arm draws the bow over the strings. And if the bowing arm position is hardly relaxed, with the elbow held fairly high, the left arm position is so tortured as to seem the invention of some fiendish inquisitor—for it is screwed around under the instrument, the elbow under the violin, in a way that looks, and sometimes *is*, agonizing. Some violinists visit osteopaths to put themselves straight. Others seek medical treatment for unpleasant sores under the chin, where the chin-rest rubs it.

This awkward position of playing was not invented, but evolved. The violin is the treble (highest) member of a string family that steadily replaced the older viols in the sixteenth century. The viols (which had frets, like the guitar) were all played in the upright position, so that even the smallest was held between the player's knees in the attitude that is used for a cello today, with the bow in the right hand and the left hand comfortably on the fingerboard and stopping the strings. But the violin's forbears were folk instruments like the pear-shaped *rebec* and the *vielle*, all of which were covered by the general name of 'fiddle'. These were held against the shoulder,

Folk fiddler in Montana at a Fourth of July celebration

though in a more relaxed way than the modern violin. At first the violin was also held fairly loosely, against the chest or resting on the shoulder. But by the eighteenth century Leopold Mozart, himself an expert violinist, was pointing out the position's inadequacies in more difficult music; and soon the grip with the chin became universal, and an actual chin-rest was fitted from the nineteenth century onwards. Nowadays a player can support the instrument by fairly light pressure between the chin and shoulder, which means that his left hand can move freely over the fingerboard.

So much for the agony. What about the ecstasy? Well, after the piano the violin is the most popular of solo instruments. Its music is vibrant and vital; it sings a song that is both intimate and tender, though it can be dramatic too with the player's right arm flashing like a swordsman's. A top performer, like Szeryng or Isaac Stern, is in demand in all the musical centres of the world; younger virtuosos such as the Korean Kyung-Wha Chung or the Italian Salvatore Accardo probably spend more than half the

The Korean violinist Kyung-Wha Chung (born 1948), is much admired for her vibrantly expressive playing

year on tour, although they always have a home base for the quiet study of new music and general practice—to say nothing of relaxation. Ruggiero Ricci has summed up the unglamorous side of the international soloist's life: 'You have to have enormous discipline. You won't find a good artist hanging around bars . . . Travelling gets worse all the time; your whole life is mapped out and it's not your own. Then you get to a place where there's absolute neglect—you arrive by train, go to the hotel, unpack, go to the rehearsal, go to the concert, go back from the concert and talk to yourself in a room and that's it. People complain about practising. So the only way you can do this: you switch on the television. Because they have a TV, for them TV is okay. You practise with the TV on and you don't get any complaints.'

The touring life has other problems. Once the members of a string quartet from eastern Europe were not on speaking terms and used to travel in separate train compartments or different parts of an aircraft. They were exceptional, but many quartet players admit that a lot of good-humoured arguing goes on in rehearsal, trying to reach a unified view of a piece. What emerges at the concert, though, must be a joint view, an interpretation influenced by four different people. Sometimes an ensemble may disintegrate as the individual members find themselves growing apart; a well-known example of this is a 'quartet' of a different kind, the Beatles. On the other hand the four members of the Amadeus String Quartet have been together since 1947, and the Beaux Arts Trio of piano, violin and cello have had only one change of personnel in twenty-five years.

The tenor member of the violin family is the viola, which is held under the chin like the violin, but is larger and tuned five notes lower. It has a more limited repertory, though it is essential in any orchestral piece and in chamber music such as string quartets. Nearly all viola players start on the violin and later take up the viola as a second instrument. Its technique is similar to the violin, though the left-hand stretches are larger.

Such stretches are more of a problem for young players of the cello—the bass of the violin family. For that reason children often learn on half- or three-

quarter-size instruments. The cello is a more comfortable instrument to learn than the violin, since the beginner can start to make a pleasant tone at a relatively early stage. It has a large solo repertory which, like the violin's, goes right back to the seventeenth century.

As with the viola, it is fairly unusual to play the double bass as a beginner's instrument. Nevertheless a young musician could take it up without having played one of the other string instruments, because the bow control is less critical than on the smaller instruments, and also because it is easier to stop the strings in the right place and thus play in tune. Despite a lot of recent music composed for it, the double bass's solo repertory is small, and it is hardly ever used in chamber music (Schubert's 'Trout' Quintet being one notable exception).

'I love talking to people with the fiddle'—so says Isaac Stern (born 1920), one of today's leading international soloists

57

Orchestral Playing

The vast majority of string performers are not soloists, but earn their living playing in chamber ensembles or, more likely still, in an orchestra. Some people like to characterize the different instruments by the temperament of the players. Are the violins really serious, or even tense, compared to the placid violas? Are the cellos jovial and pub-going, 'an irresponsible, cheerful lot', as Bernard Shore says in his book *The Orchestra Speaks*? And are the double basses really dog kennels whose proud owners treat them to excessive 'spit and polish', looking scornfully at the cellos when a conductor says the lower strings are out of tune? Probably all of this is half accurate, generally true but no more. Orchestral players are usually good-tempered and (what is more) thoroughly professional. The player turns up on time for a rehearsal, recording session or concert, gets his instrument out and warmed up without fuss, plays well, packs up and goes home. If he chats to his neighbour it is more likely to be about his vegetable garden or the Test Match score than about the music. He is a performer for whom first-rate playing is routine.

A string quartet includes two violins, viola and cello. Pictured here is the Allegri String Quartet

As for the orchestral player's attitude to the conductor, he accepts him as an ally and sees no reason to be frightened by him. Sometimes a conductor will bring a special magnetism, an 'electricity' to a performance and the players are aware and responsive to this. But whatever the conductor's contribution, the orchestra can give an adequate account of the music. Once in Beethoven's Fifth Symphony a conductor's braces snapped during the first movement and for the rest of the work the unfortunate maestro was more concerned to keep his trousers up than to give a great interpretation; but, in the words of one of the orchestral violinists, it was still 'a grand professional performance'.

Orchestral players nowadays—at least in the big centres—are no longer the slaves of tyrannical conductors who can dismiss them at will. In fact the boot is almost entirely on the other foot. The London Symphony Orchestra, for example, is democratically run by the players. They themselves have the power to 'hire and fire' a conductor. On the other hand, they also have the painful task of dismissing their own fellow players where declining abilities or temperamental problems make this necessary.

The Guitar

The guitar is a string instrument that we associate with solo music. There are no guitar parts in works for symphony orchestra. On the other hand, in pop music the guitar—the electric guitar, not the classical Spanish instrument—is an essential part of any group.

The guitar belongs to an instrumental family that goes back into the depths of the ancient world. The Greek *kithara* was a lyre, without the 'body' of the guitar; but the related words *kithara*, zither, cittern and even the Welsh *crwth* all refer to string instruments that are plucked rather than bowed. It was played in Restoration England by the future King James II, but by the nineteenth century it was associated especially with Spain. Almost alone, the Spanish guitarist Andrés Segovia (born in 1893) brought it from its folk and domestic status into the concert hall. Nowadays there are fine guitarists of all nationalities. The Englishman Julian Bream is

Duo for guitar and lute:
John Williams (left) and
Julian Bream

among the foremost of these today. When he was a
student in London he was forbidden to take his guitar
into the college of music where he studied the piano
and cello, for the guitar was not considered a serious
instrument at all at that time, around 1950. But he
persevered, with Segovia's encouragement, and quite
soon he was established as a virtuoso of international
standard, on both the guitar and the lute. Bream has
persuaded composers to write for the guitar and so
enlarged its repertory: nowadays guitar music is no
longer confined to Spanish or 'pseudo-Spanish'
pieces and 'arrangements' from Bach. Benjamin
Britten composed a *Nocturnal* for Bream. There is a
story of how, over lunch, Britten asked the guitarist
if he could play a certain chord. Bream looked at it
and said 'no'. 'Try it when you get home,' Britten
urged. 'I got out the old guitar,' says Bream, 'and . . .
the bastard!' Thus composers sometimes extend even
a great performer's technique. Another British
guitarist, John Williams, has also had music written
specially for him, like Stephen Dodgson's concerto;
and he has recorded two-guitar music with Julian
Bream. Recently he has moved into the more popular
field as a member of the group *Sky*.

If you are wanting to take up the guitar you may be
thinking of using it to accompany folk songs or to
play in a pop group. Both of these are important uses
of the guitar, of course; but it is worth considering
learning the classical Spanish guitar first, since this

60

Osian Ellis, playing at
Benjamin Britten's
Aldeburgh Festival in
1978

will give you a strong and versatile technique and teach you how to read music. It is then quite easy to transfer to other styles of music, in which only a kind of musical shorthand—like chord symbols—may be used. It is much harder to transfer in the other direction!

The Harp

For a while the harp seemed to be associated with women performers. Sidonie Goosens has played for no less than fifty years in the BBC Symphony Orchestra, though she is still graceful and youthful-looking. But today it is Osian Ellis who is perhaps the leading British player. He was brought up on the traditional music of his native Wales, which includes a long tradition of harp playing. Dr Ellis (he was so honoured by the University of Wales in 1970) thinks the harp began with the bow and arrow—'the early huntsman strummed his string, and it made a musical sound'—and he has reminded us that it is found nearly everywhere in the world. The modern harp, with its soundboard and pedals, is quite a large and heavy instrument (weighing nearly a hundred-weight, it is heavier than a double bass), and a very expensive one too. Apart from being awkward to carry, its forty-seven strings, mainly of gut, are very sensitive to the humidity of the atmosphere. It can take a long time to tune before a concert, and then go out of tune again when the main lights are switched on, so that it is best to tune quickly at the last minute. Like Bream, Osian Ellis had a work specially written for him by Benjamin Britten, a Harp Suite; Britten used the harp a lot in his music and extended its technical and expressive resources quite considerably.

How does one begin on the harp? Osian Ellis was lucky enough to be brought up in a home where it was played. Otherwise it is probably best to start on the piano, where you can at least see the notes clearly and so learn more quickly to read music. (With the harp the strings are close to the player's face, and also close to each other. The C and F strings are coloured so that the harpist knows where he is.) A small Irish harp or *clarsach* would be the next stage, before going on to the large and more elaborate harp of the symphony orchestra.

Finale

And how does it feel to be a string player, whether a soloist or in an orchestra? A dozen performers might give a dozen different answers. 'Very often I feel I could give it up because it is quite a hard life,' Osian Ellis says. 'The only way really to cope is when you are on top of the world ... you enjoy playing something sometimes and on another day you might be quite nervous with the same tune ... although you may have qualms about giving a performance, the best way is to say: "Here it is, let's hope it will be all right!"' The orchestral violinist Dennis Simons says: 'I think you do it because you have to do it. So you have terrific motivation to start with, which keeps you practising and all the rest of it. And I think if you didn't enjoy performing you'd very soon give it up and do something else, because it is too difficult—it's similar to being a sportsman ... you get the adrenalin going and things start to happen, and then you perform.' And the viola player Alan Smyth, of the London Symphony Orchestra: 'I just like playing, and I like the varied life that I have now, and I love the music. And by that I mean all kinds of music, not just great music ... I just like pulling the bow across the strings.' The great violinist Isaac Stern has said, simply yet eloquently: 'I love talking to people with the fiddle'.

The Wind Performers

7

The Recorder

The recorder is not an orchestral instrument today, for it died out early in the eighteenth century before the modern orchestra developed. However, it is worth discussing here since it has been revived and is perhaps the most common instrument taken up by children, particularly in junior schools. This has resulted in its being associated with childish music-making, which is unfortunate since in the hands of a skilled player like the Dutchman Frans Brueggen the recorder can be a beautiful and versatile instrument. Furthermore, it has a large repertory of music from medieval, Renaissance and Baroque times, including Bach's 2nd and 4th Brandenburg Concertos.

So if you have learned the recorder at school, you need not necessarily give it up in favour of a more 'grown-up' instrument. With 'early music' now an established part of the musical scene there are teachers who can help you progress. And you need not learn only the recorder: its fingering is similar in many ways to that of the oboe and bassoon, and these are therefore good instruments to learn at the same time or to move on to.

Orchestral Woodwind

The woodwind in the modern symphony orchestra consists of flutes, oboes, clarinets and bassoons; there are normally two of each. In the larger works of

In this orchestral wind section we see woodwind instruments ranging from piccolos (centre left) to double bassoon (centre right). The flute itself is not illustrated, since both flautists are playing piccolo at this point in the music

the nineteenth and twentieth centuries more may be used, together with related instruments: the piccolo (a small flute), cor anglais (large oboe), bass clarinet and the deep-toned double bassoon.

The Flute

The flautist, or flutist, is one of the most versatile of musicians. A player was once asked if he could understand a sign written in Chinese and answered, 'No, but I think I could play it if I had my flute.' Poets talk of the 'soft complaining flute' and many composers have featured it in pastoral and amorous music. Yet the woman flautist Atarah Ben-Tovim has said that you need 'a fantastic strong body, tremendous strong belly muscles, tremendous strong teeth and mouth . . . as a professional instrument it can be torture'. Still, the London Symphony Orchestra's Peter Lloyd started on the flute as a boy because he was asthmatic—a case of kill or cure perhaps!

With its breathy tone, the flute often wears an aura of mystery; like the solo that begins Debussy's *The Afternoon of a Faun.* No wonder it is associated with the Greek god Pan and the haunted noonday of ancient Arcadia. The humorist Paul Jennings has put it beautifully. Flautists, he says, are the most mysterious people in the orchestra, 'inscrutable-looking men called Rogers or Morris . . . The orchestra stops banging and roaring, it hangs a quiet

64

curtain of chords for them—and with half-closed eyes they play their warbling solos, the hall dissolves into a shimmering sunlit glade . . .' Sir Malcolm Sargent, the conductor, told of a woman whom the sound of a flute always sent into hysterics. And there was the Pied Piper of Hamelin, whose enchantment led the children of the town away.

'The man with the golden flute', James Galway

Some of that fascination remains. James Galway, a brilliant Irish flautist who looks like a twinkling leprechaun, gave up his post as principal flute with the Berlin Philharmonic Orchestra and became a popular solo artist. His tune *Annie's Song* reached the hit parade and he became the 'Man with the Golden Flute' and a regular television performer. Atarah Ben-Tovim similarly gave up orchestral playing and started her own group, Atarah's Band. A lady of immense gusto and skill, she tours with her flute and her musicians and gives not so much

65

concerts as musical parties for children—here is a modern Pied Piper, and though the children fortunately don't disappear they do remember the enchantment of her music.

The Oboe

Oboists are different, like their instrument: sometimes they even seem physically thinner, in keeping with the reedy tone of the 'poignant, plangent oboe'. Though it can be agile enough, the oboe seems to tempt composers into writing smooth, expressive music. The Swiss oboist Heinz Holliger says that he tries to make his instrument as expressive as the violin or even the human voice, and his especially rich tonal variety has encouraged composers to write for him in ways that extend traditional oboe technique: for that matter he is himself a composer. As with the clarinet and bassoon, the tone depends crucially upon the reeds (of which the oboe, like the bassoon, has two). Holliger prepares his own: 'I hate scraping reeds, it's really the nastiest bit of oboe playing. Without reeds the oboe would be a very nice instrument.' A love-hate relationship, one might think, between the player and his instrument; more love than hate, though, to judge from the exquisite sound the oboe can make in the hands of a good player.

Beginners on the oboe, however, do have their troubles. A poor posture can cause agonizing breathing problems, for the oboist must be able to breathe deeply. And though the oboe may give the note A for an orchestra to tune to, good tuning is hard to achieve even for a professional performer with a first-rate instrument (some keys, like E major, are 'a devil'), so that a student who plays his scales well in tune shows promise. For that reason the oboe is not really a good choice as a first instrument for a musical beginner at school. It is better as a second instrument, say for a pianist or recorder player with musicianship and with some years experience—and, in addition, who can learn on an instrument of fairly good quality.

The Clarinet

By contrast, the early stages of clarinet playing are

encouraging. It starts (at least) by being easy: you can make a reasonable sound quickly, more easily than with the flute or the oboe. A beginner on the oboe all too often sounds like the proverbial 'dying duck in a thunderstorm', but though a clarinettist too can squawk and squeak the instrument is more controllable in tone and also in intonation (tuning); a relatively inexpensive clarinet, too, will give a better result than a cheap oboe.

The clarinettist Gervase de Peyer echoes Heinz Holliger's remarks about the oboe when he says that he aims at a suppleness like that of the human voice. Again, much depends on the reed (the clarinet has only one), which is probably imported from France (even though the instrument itself may be English) and even then has to be worked on with sandpaper or a delicate knife. (Although reeds can be made of glass fibre or other artificial material, they are normally of cane, the *sativa* grass that grows on the Mediterranean coast.) Lip technique—called *embouchure*—depends on the player's own physical attributes. The young musician with uneven teeth should probably avoid taking up a reed wind instrument. Small or weak hands and poor lung capacity are also handicaps. Playing the clarinet, or any other wind instrument, is a physical activity; yet often such points are not taken into consideration, even by teachers, when a boy or girl thinks of taking up an instrument.

The Bassoon

Whoever wants to take up the bassoon must face some problems. The instrument, large and with many keys to cover holes that the fingers cannot reach, is expensive. The cheapest instrument stocked by Boosey & Hawkes costs (in late 1980) £655 ($1600) and comes from Czechoslovakia, while an American bassoon is £905 ($2,200). Its solo repertory is limited, although Mozart and Weber wrote bassoon concertos and Saint-Saëns a bassoon sonata. It is tricky to play: it is the only instrument among the woodwind that uses all ten fingers, and 'the thumb has to fly around in all directions', as one professional player admits. Another, William Waterhouse, has said frankly that you need a sense of humour to play the

bassoon. Not just because people tend to be amused by its plump yet reedy sound—so suitable for 'granddad' in Prokofiev's *Peter and the Wolf*—but also to cope with the demands composers frequently make on an instrument that can be 'intractable'— hard to deal with, that is, like a not very docile animal.

Opposite: Clarinets (foreground) and bassoons

The Saxophone

The saxophone was developed in about 1840 by the Belgian wind instrument designer Adolphe Sax, but has never found a regular place in the symphony orchestra. It does not really blend well with other wind instruments, though a few composers have used its very individual sound to good effect—such as Ravel in his arrangement of Mussorgsky's *Pictures at an Exhibition*. Recently ensembles like the London Saxophone Quartet have encouraged composers to write new music for the instrument. Nevertheless, it is with jazz and swing that the instrument is mainly associated, and most people who learn it will be aiming at those fields. The technique of the instrument is close to the clarinet, which it resembles in having a single reed. There are four sizes, soprano, alto, tenor and bass, of which the alto and tenor are most commonly used.

Saxophone to the fore, bass on the floor: a swinging picture of Bill Haley and his Comets, touring Britain in 1957

Brass Instruments

The trumpet is the treble member of the family of brass instruments used in a symphony orchestra. It has tonal grandeur and much agility—for example, it can produce rapid repeated notes—but, as with all brass instruments, the player's embouchure is all-important. Nevertheless young players, girls as well as boys, often take up the trumpet with success. Some come to it through the easier cornet, the treble instrument in brass bands. The tone of the trumpet is, of course, prominent, and a fluffed 'attack', to say nothing of a wrong note, cannot go unnoticed; so even an orchestral player is a soloist to some extent and needs a solo player's temperament, with the ability to keep going even when things are not going well. If trumpet players usually seem 'cool, calm and collected', this is because real nerves would in-

'Dizzy' Gillespie (born 1917) plays brilliant jazz trumpet and uses a special instrument with up-turned bell, here played with a mute right up against the microphone

evitably affect the breathing and embouchure, and thus the tone and probably also the rhythm. The trumpet's tone quality is itself so assured and confident that the performer dare not allow uncertainty to creep into what he is playing.

The trombone may be still easier than the trumpet as a beginner's instrument. It is not really difficult to make a delicate and lyrical sound, although this may surprise people who only associate the trombones with massive orchestral climaxes. But like every brass performer, the trombonist in an orchestra needs stamina, a good lip technique and strong lungs, to get through a concert; his playing cannot be allowed to deteriorate during the evening, particularly when the final item on the programme is likely to be some orchestral showpiece whose technical demands are the greatest of the evening.

The deepest instrument in the brass family is the tuba. This instrument has a slightly comic image with its fat 'Tubby the Tuba' tonal quality. It provides the bass for the brass family without, unfortunately, quite blending with the trumpets and trombones, because of its rounder tone. The tuba player has not much in the way of a solo repertory, though there is a concerto by the English composer Vaughan Williams. Nevertheless there are tuba players whose technical skill is of a high enough order to deserve the word virtuosity. One such player, John Fletcher, has remarked rather ruefully that the instrument 'has its own body language'; what he means, among other things, is that an inexperienced person carrying a tuba might easily fall and injure himself.

The horn is perhaps the most important solo brass instrument. At one time it was also the most difficult. Until the time of the exceptionally skilled British player Dennis Brain (tragically killed in a motoring accident at the age of thirty-six in 1957) no-one altogether expected a horn player to possess the technical security of a trumpeter. But in the last twenty years, and especially since the general adoption of the four-valved 'double horn' that facilitates the performance of high notes, horn players are as secure as any other brass player— which is just as well, since composers make enormous demands on their skill. There are now women horn players as well as men. After all, there is no reason why their breathing technique and embouchure should not be as sure; and at least they do not have the male wind players' nightmare of cutting themselves shaving and being out of action on the day of an important concert. (It is often forgotten what a disastrous effect a cough, sneezing or a runny nose has on a wind player!) 'I try not to allow my nerves to go through the instrument,' one player has said; 'you may want to cough, but you have to control it.'

Brass Bands

The British brass band movement goes back to the 1830s, the first band probably being that of the Blaina Ironworks in Wales, founded in 1832. They are not

A local brass band
marching along the
'Romantic Road' in
southern Germany
which passes through
old towns such as
Nuremberg

military bands, though similar to them in some ways. The instruments are brass and percussion—cornets (rather than trumpets) and saxhorns, euphoniums and 'bombardons' (tubas), cymbals and drums. The lead cornet player is like the leader of a symphony orchestra and is entrusted with important solos. His position is one of honour and the conductor will do well to 'keep on the right side' of him.

The brass band tradition is especially strong nowadays in Yorkshire and Lancashire, where a particular band is usually associated with a factory, or perhaps a colliery. There may be about three thousand such bands in existence today—roughly 60,000 players therefore, all amateurs and playing mainly for their own satisfaction. But these amateurs take the brass band movement very seriously, and competitively—there are national contests where to win a prize is a matter of local pride. Sometimes bands branch out into something new. In 1978 the Brighouse and Rastrick Colliery Band got into the British hit parade with its version of the Cornish *Floral Dance*, while in 1973 the Grimethorpe Colliery Band broke new ground by having an avant-garde piece written for them by Harrison Birtwistle. A recent television film, *Shillingbury Blowers*, depicted a fictional band, reflecting the interest that still exists nationally in this kind of music-making. Brass bands offer splendid opportunities for school-age musicians of both sexes who are lucky enough to live in those parts of Britain where the tradition is strong. In America, brass bands were popular in the mid-nineteenth century—there was a 'Gilmore's Grand Boston Band' formed in 1859—but the tradition has not been kept up as in Britain.

8

Sue Addison
At Work in an Orchestra

Sue Addison

Sue Addison is petite, attractive and full of enthusiasm. She's successful, too, for she's a member of the City of Birmingham Symphony Orchestra, which in such a competitive profession is no mean feat at twenty-five years of age. But the most surprising thing about Sue, particularly in view of her size, is her choice of instrument—she plays the trombone.

It requires a great deal of physical stamina to play as Sue readily admits.

'You need to put in a tremendous amount of wind, especially in an orchestra when the trombone sometimes has to be very forceful to overpower some of the other members. So you need to be very fit to put the actual amount of air through the instrument.'

Sue didn't have a burning ambition to play the trombone. In fact she wanted to learn the piano as a child but her family couldn't afford the lessons. So she had to wait until she was about fourteen before she could have any music tuition at all, and this was through the school orchestra.

'By that time I'd have liked to have studied the flute or clarinet,' she recalls, 'but there was a waiting list for them as there was a limited number available at the school. Violins were always free but I knew I was very old to start on such a difficult instrument. So I took the only other thing that was there, and that was the trombone!'

Sue's talent must have become obvious very

74

quickly because she was awarded a special grant when she was sixteen by her education authority to attend a sixth form college some distance away so that she could have special coaching on the trombone. She attributes much of this progress to the local amateur brass band that she joined only six weeks after she first took up trombone.

Sue Addison (right) plays her trombone during a lunchtime recital of a brass quintet at the Royal College of Music, London

'They gave me so much encouragement because they made me see the purpose of practice through the enjoyment of playing. As an adult band they were also of a much higher standard than I was which made me work hard to improve, and their repertoire gave me my interest in music.'

She was so keen that she used to practise for about an hour a day. Most young people only do about half an hour when they first start because of the strenuous nature of the instrument.

'But I was always asked to practise it sitting down because you can get quite short-winded and dizzy,' she adds.

Although she took the required Associated Board Examination at Grade Eight to apply to music college, Sue thinks her experience with the brass band was by far the most valuable training she could have had at that stage.

75

'There's a lot to be said for exams, of course, but just working for them and churning out set pieces is not enough. The child is not seeing enough music, and reading music is the thing. The more you read the better you get and this only comes through playing.'

This certainly paid off in Sue's case because after an audition she was accepted by the Royal College of Music. She says that although the audition was terrifying, you are never judged solely on your performance—it's potential they're looking for.

'I hadn't been playing seriously for very long— about three and a half years—so I can't imagine that they went on my playing abilities then.'

She had marvellous tuition at the college in both chamber and orchestral music. But she says one of the most valuable things about being a student is that you get the opportunity to play and without that it will be almost impossible to find work later. And if there are too many students for you to get into one of the official college orchestras or groups then you can always start your own.

'I gained my experience by setting up groups with other people at college, like brass quintets and trombone quartets or trios. Playing with other people makes you listen—something that practising on your own for hours can't do. I think more stress should be put on ear training because you've got to be taught to listen, and playing as much as possible is the only way.'

Sue doesn't underestimate practice either though and points out that college is the only opportunity you have to do as much as you really want or need because once you're working regularly there just isn't enough time. Through college you also make contacts which become vital once you start looking for work. So much relies on personal recommendation—because it's such a closed little world your name gets round by word of mouth. It's a good idea therefore to start building your reputation through freelance work while you're still a student.

Sue left the Royal College after four years with her ARCM—(Associate of the Royal College of Music) and although she claims that the qualification itself doesn't actually get you a job, it enabled her to teach privately and part-time in schools when she was

Relaxing in Rome while
on tour with the
London Cornett and
Sackbut Ensemble

short of money.

'To get an audition with an orchestra, it's not the
qualification they're interested in but what you've
done and which scholarships, awards and prizes you
won at college.'

People in the music business often know what
vacancies are about to come up before they're
advertised in the press, and naturally with so many
musicians out of work, large numbers apply for each
job—Sue says forty-seven applied for her present
post.

If you are invited to an audition you will have to
play a couple of pieces—sometimes set and sometimes of your own choice—in front of a panel. You
will also be given some sightreading tests, which is
when past playing experience really helps.

'It's a very tedious process for the panel,' Sue says.
'They're probably there all day listening to players
and sometimes all the next day too. It's very difficult,
but I can't see any fairer system really.'

Once you've passed the audition you are put on a
trial period with the orchestra which can vary from
weeks to months.

'Normally they make you feel quite at home
because they realize you're under pressure. They just
try and make you feel relaxed. I did about a month's
trial for the City of Birmingham Symphony Orchestra and I didn't hear whether I'd got the job for
about three months because they had eight or nine

other people to try.'

The conditions of a contract vary from orchestra to orchestra but you do have to work a certain number of hours per year. Yet you still get lots of free time to do other work and sometimes—at the discretion of the section—you can even miss a concert if you've got a particularly important freelance date. At other times when the music of composers like Mozart and Beethoven doesn't include trombones, Sue is obviously not needed. For her one of the attractions of the work is this lack of routine.

'There's no concert on the same day every week. Some weeks we could be working only two days and another week six. Sometimes we tour and sometimes we make records—and the rehearsal schedule is equally erratic.'

So Sue manages a fair amount of freelance work between commitments—in fact before her job in Birmingham she had been freelance since she was at college. She plays with various Baroque groups (sometimes on a medieval version of the trombone called a sackbut) and brass groups.

'I enjoy it because I think it's more intimate with smaller ensembles. But I must say that since I've played with the orchestra I've also developed a love for very loud music and that feeling of tremendous power that this can give, especially when composers like Mahler, Bruckner and Stravinsky write for seventy or eighty players.'

She freelances with other orchestras, too, when somebody is ill or away and occasionally when composers have written for extra brass. But she doesn't have to for financial reasons. As a single person she says her income from the orchestra is sufficient, although other players with families often *have* to supplement their incomes. (Salaries in Britain are relatively low.)

Despite the security that comes with being a full-time orchestra member, Sue thinks that one day she'd either like to move to a London orchestra or go completely freelance again.

'Some players in the orchestra are satisfied with the job there but I travel around and do other work as well because I like to travel abroad and meet different people. It makes me very busy but I don't mind because I have no commitments at the moment—I'm single. But if I do take on other commitments then I might find full-time freelancing better because I could then say yes or no to each individual job, I wouldn't be working to a contract.'

The orchestra uses a lot of guest conductors and Sue thinks that the quality of the conducting greatly affects a performance. Even when the orchestra is very experienced and can cope with the piece, if the conductor is bad the music won't have that vital flair. She agrees that conducting is a very difficult job.

'A conductor not only has to be good technically but he's got to be very good at handling musicians. If he doesn't click with the players for some reason and they get fed up then it is reflected in their performance.'

She believes that most players feel nervous before a concert, although she confesses that she is even more on edge when she's playing in a smaller group and is more exposed, or when she's playing a solo or a particularly difficult piece. Sue also warns that after a concert you must occasionally be prepared for disappointment.

'I feel quite distressed if something's gone very badly. You've got to play as a unit and if the unit works well then I get the most satisfaction. If the unit hasn't played particularly well but I've managed to cope myself then I don't feel quite so depressed. But if the unit plays well, you've practised very hard and travelled miles—this is usually in small groups— then it's very disheartening if only a handful of people show up. It's difficult but you've got to play your best regardless—you just have to concentrate on the music and try to overcome your disappointment.'

Sue stresses that as a profession it's not all roses. 'It's hard work and often you're doing it all for very little money. But it's the job satisfaction that's the most important thing,' and there must be more of that than in most jobs.

In Britain you really have to be a member of the Musicians' Union to work, but unlike the actor's union, it's not difficult to join. Sue says a telephone is another necessity for a musician because often work comes up at the last minute. She herself has an

answering machine because so many jobs are lost by just being out.

Sue adds further variety to her life by teaching a few private pupils which, as a part-time activity, she enjoys.

'I like to give something else to the profession and it can be just as rewarding if you've got a keen pupil who's doing well and making progress as it is to sit in front of an audience.'

She has also done a certain amount of session work in the past, but found it a bit soul-destroying sitting in a box playing into a microphone.

'A lot of session musicians miss the "vibes" you get from a live audience and so they play in small groups in pubs and clubs for a pittance in the evenings just to play the sort of music they really love.'

Her advice to up-and-coming young musicians is uncompromising and based on criteria that she has obviously set for herself.

'Practise! Work hard! If you want to be a musician, you've got to be committed because there's no easy way into the profession. You also have to keep fit— particularly wind and brass players—and because the hours are irregular and the travelling can get quite exhausting, you can become very rundown. If you're physically fit it affects you mentally too.'

She also thinks discipline is very important because when you're out of work and feeling depressed you've still got to find the enthusiasm to practise. One way round this is again to form your own group or enter competitions just so that you have something to work for. But ultimately, in Sue's opinion, a combination of talent and drive will be successful.

'You've got to have the determination, be able to take the knocks and disappointments. You must be strong-willed and not too introverted because you need a personality to put over the music to the audience. Also it's very important that you get on with other people, for musicians have to work together very closely.

'It's not always the most outstandingly talented player who makes it—there must be ambition too.'

Opposite: The conductor Simon Rattle bows at the end of a concert given by the City of Birmingham Symphony Orchestra. Sue is among the brass players, a little above the centre of the picture

9 Keyboards and Percussion

The Piano Players

Piano players are the personality performers among the instrumentalists. The pianist, unlike the string or wind player, most often performs entirely alone; but he and his instrument can fill a large hall such as London's Royal Festival Hall with its seating capacity of over three thousand—just as he can also play in a small salon holding fifty people as Chopin did in the nineteenth century.

Though the piano repertory only covers about two hundred years of music, from Mozart's time to the present day, it is very large. The Romantic composers, as we have seen, loved the piano, which was both personal and poetic in a way that stimulated their imagination. Beethoven's thirty-two piano sonatas opened up the way for the piano music of Schubert, Mendelssohn, Chopin, Liszt, Brahms and

The great pianist Artur Rubinstein brings much warmth of personality to the music he plays

others, right up to Ravel and Rachmaninov in the twentieth century. Pianists never run out of things to learn; indeed one of the main tasks of a piano student is to get at least the instrument's most important pieces into his head. Literally 'into his head'—for unlike players of other instruments, recital pianists since Liszt commonly play from memory. It is worth considering this demand, really only made of pianists—to play a whole concert entirely by heart and entirely alone. If you falter the music itself stumbles or stops, for there can be no 'prompter' offstage for a musical performance. Some pianists therefore have had extraordinary gifts of memory. Claudio Arrau, as a young man, is supposed to have been able to play any one of seventy different programmes at a moment's notice.

Another problem that must be faced by any pianist is that he has to play whatever instrument is available. There have been a few players who insisted on travelling with their own grand piano. The Italian Arturo Benedetti Michelangeli is one of these, whose extremely well-maintained instrument reputedly has its action (mechanism) tailored specially to his requirements. But things can go wrong. One recital Michelangeli was to give at the Royal Festival Hall in London was cancelled at a few hours' notice because the piano had been damaged in transit and the artist was unwilling to accept a substitute. Otherwise, a pianist simply has to get the very best out of the instrument that is in the hall. For he knows that if it sounds badly, it is he, rather than the piano, that is likely to be blamed. Imagine how a singer would feel if asked to use an unknown set of vocal chords belonging to someone else, or a violinist to play an instrument not his own!

Star Pianists

After Franz Liszt, the most successful pianist was probably the Pole Ignacy Paderewski (1860–1941). In his fifty years before the public he earned an enormous sum of money. He travelled in a private railway carriage, with a chef, butler, masseur and physician—plus his wife and her aides as well—so that his tours were like royal processions. He looked romantic too. The English painter Sir Edward Burne-

Jones took one look at Paderewski and told his friends he had seen an archangel walking the earth: he then painted a famous portrait. This pianist's golden-red hair amused the caricaturists but delighted his admirers, and he was pursued by innumerable young girls like the teeny-boppers of today's pop scene. Even towards the end of his career, when the critics noted all kinds of inaccuracies in his playing, people fought at the doors to get into his concerts. Such was his popularity that he was actually elected prime minister of Poland in 1919.

Rachmaninov, Rubinstein, Horowitz—these are great names of the next couple of generations after Paderewski. Sergei Rachmaninov came to professional piano performance when over forty, after he left Russia at the time of the 1917 Revolution. A tall, unsmiling figure with a colossal technique, his playing was both virile and subtle. Some people called his style 'imperial', while others talked of its 'purity'.

Artur Rubinstein, from Poland, is a *bon viveur* by comparison with Rachmaninov, a lover of beautiful women and beautiful music alike, whose playing— perhaps especially in his beloved Chopin—has warmth and spontaneity. Rubinstein's relaxed

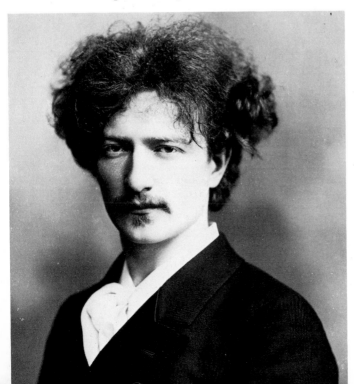

Paderewski, the Romantic Polish pianist with his famous mop of hair

approach permitted him a career of no less than seventy years, without the decline in technique suffered by some other pianists—a unique record. Now in his nineties and living mainly in Paris, he still seems to possess the secret of truly joyful living that has always seemed to inform his pianistic art.

Vladimir Horowitz, a Russian born in 1904, is different again. He has been called an introvert compared to Rubinstein. 'A million volts of technique,' people have said, and that frightening energy implies—literally—high tension, 'a demon trying to get loose', thrilling but disturbing. But for all the electricity in Horowitz's playing, he can relax and play with unaffected simplicity when he wants to. A Chopin mazurka or Debussy prelude, especially when he is in the quiet of a recording studio, shows Horowitz in a gentle and intimate mood—the opposite of the flashing, almost aggressive style in his famous 1941 performance of the Tchaikovsky First Concerto with Toscanini conducting.

Piano Professionals Today

Pianists are nearly always soloists. The violinist who does not 'make it' as a soloist can work in an orchestra or in a chamber ensemble; but for the pianist it is often a case of 'all or nothing', though he can become an accompanist if his talents lie in that direction. It is hard for a pianist, compared (say) to a harp or tuba player, to get into a college of music or conservatory today, and even among those who do there is an alarming drop-out rate as talented young musicians realize that earning a living just by playing the piano is very difficult. Many compromise and do part-time teaching which may gradually become more like a full-time occupation; some are deeply disillusioned and leave music altogether. International competitions like those at Warsaw and Leeds show today's very high standards: some of these young pianists seem incapable of playing a wrong note, and yet only the outright winners are assured of an international career. It is not so much in Britain as in Russia and other eastern European countries that intensive technical and interpretative training begins early enough to ensure this kind of pianistic assurance—though France and America

The 1978 Tchaikovsky Competition in Moscow, dominated by a picture of the composer. The competitor is Gail Martin of the USA

too have produced outstanding young talents. Some pianists who do make the grade still find the pace uncomfortably hot and have a love-hate relationship with the instrument; some lucky ones just enjoy it; others like Stephen Bishop-Kovacevich find the pianist's life 'addictive, appearing before a public'. Certain things, like the available piano or the acoustics of a hall, are doubtless outside the pianist's control and must be accepted for better or worse— otherwise 'rest, preparation, confidence' are the things to aim for. And with today's intensive touring, family life is hard. The accompanist Antony Saunders has said that 'it is very hard to be a dedicated musician and not be utterly selfish' and that if you don't work out some pattern of family living that balances marriage and music 'you end up with a marriage that doesn't work, or a non-career as a musician'. The Muse is a very demanding lady!

The Harpsichord

This instrument is the forerunner of the piano and became obsolete in the nineteenth century as the piano took over. Its repertory covers about three centuries from 1500—more than the piano's—and as this music has been rediscovered the harpsichord has been revived. It is now regarded as a fully developed instrument in its own right, not as a kind of poor relation of the piano.

The harpsichord's keyboard is like that of a piano, but its strings are plucked by a plectrum of quill or leather. Harpsichord players have nearly always learned piano or organ initially—perhaps because of the scarcity and expense of harpsichords. But today more and more schools are buying instruments; and firms like Zuckermann in America are producing fine harpsichords in kit form, so that you can build your own instrument for no more than the cost of an upright piano. Certainly it is an attractive choice of keyboard instrument if your tastes are mainly in Renaissance and Baroque music. Unlike the pipe organ, it is one that you can have in your own home!

The Organ

Organists almost always start learning in church, which is generally where organs are to be found. That

Vladimir Ashkenazy (born 1937) was joint first prizewinner of the Tchaikovsky Competition in 1962. His warm temperament and magnificently groomed technique have made him a leader among the pianists of his generation

The organ at Eisenstadt, Austria, which Haydn used to play during his many years of service to the Esterházy family

means a repertory of J. S. Bach, César Franck, respectable English composers, perhaps something modern like Olivier Messaien . . . and more Bach. It is inevitably a more sober, and perhaps limited repertory, than the piano's—who, for example, plays dance music on the organ, whether ancient or modern?

Yet there have been organ virtuosos, like the Italians Merulo and Frescobaldi already mentioned. Bach and some of his predecessors attracted audiences too with brilliant music. Handel wrote, and played, organ concertos which might be heard in a theatre rather than a church. The Royal Albert Hall organ in London, an instrument with ten thousand pipes built in 1871, still thrills audiences today. Cinema organists in the early twentieth century delighted filmgoers between the two world wars. In America there is a vast instrument in Atlantic City, New Jersey, in an auditorium seating 41,000 people. One of its two consoles has a record seven keyboards (or 'manuals'). There is a 'showbiz' element where such colossal instruments are concerned. One young American organist, Carlo Curley (born in 1952), has emerged in the last decade as a quite unashamed popularizer of the organ, stripping away from it what he considers unnecessary veils of awe. He plays to large audiences, makes records in which Scott Joplin's *The Entertainer* goes alongside a Bach chorale prelude and Sousa's *Washington Post March* complements Handel's *Hallelujah Chorus*, and he tours with his own electronic instrument.

The Synthesizer

An electronic organ, like the Hammond organ which has been available since 1935, has no pipes, nor of course does it need wind pressure. It is therefore as compact as an upright piano, though it needs a loudspeaker. Electric oscillations are generated and a variety of tone colours (or timbres) are produced. A synthesizer is in many ways simply a very advanced version of the same thing, 'creating' sounds that are not pre-set as with the electronic organ but really infinitely variable. It can be played like an organ, with its keyboard, or can put music directly on to multi-track tape. A synthesizer performance, such as those of Bach by Walter Carlos or the Debussy piano music recreated by the Japanese performer Isao Tomita, is sometimes an elaborate instrumentation that is built up layer by layer on tape. It therefore cannot take place 'live' but belongs in the recording studio. But the synthesizer can play directly also, and its fascinating range of sounds, different from those produced by any earlier keyboard instrument, have found their place in music, though not yet in the symphony orchestra.

Percussion

Some percussion instruments have a keyboard. The celesta, for example, is like a short-keyboard piano with metal bars instead of strings. Others, like the xylophone with its wooden bars of differing lengths, have a sort of 'keyboard' except that the notes are struck with beaters. On the other hand, the drums, cymbals, castanets and so on are of a different construction altogether and, with the exception of the timpani, do not produce definite notes. But all percussion instruments are struck in some way—for that is what the word means.

The percussion might seem modern; we perhaps associate it with jazz, or pop music with its heavy beat, or military bands. But percussion instruments

Assorted percussion, photographed in a recording studio. The screens are placed by the engineers for acoustic reasons

go back into the depths of antiquity. The Sumerians had a big drum over 2000 years B.C., for example. And medieval illustrations are full of percussion instruments—not surprisingly, after all, since music was then often played in the open air and used for dancing. In Africa drums are still associated with magic, and used to send signals.

Today's western percussion players, though, are far from being merely time-beaters. The percussion department in a symphony orchestra includes a large range of tone colours and can produce effects which are gentle and subtle as well as the earthquakes of sound required in such a work as Stravinsky's *The Rite of Spring*. They are sometimes even asked to concoct sounds as a perfumer might create a new scent by blending ingredients—anything from seashore noises to an atomic explosion, perhaps in the context of a film or a television advertisement. One of England's senior players, James Blades, has spoken of the constant, almost primitive satisfaction that he gets from his work, even after a lifetime's playing: 'Drumming is a great business, you know. I come into this little studio that we're in, and hour after hour I can sit and play this drum.' And a younger player, Keith Millar of the London Philharmonic Orchestra, can still say at the age of thirty-four: 'it still seems like a game, like fun—I hope it will always stay that way'.

Sometimes the percussionist has his frustrations. In a symphony by Bruckner he may be on stage for over an hour yet actually play only a few notes. Yet because of their very rarity those notes will, and must, be telling. Woe betide the unfortunate musician who plays his single cymbal clash before—or after—the great climax where it is due and which the composer has built up perhaps over several minutes of music! Some percussion technique is tricky, like the side drum roll and the thumb roll on the

The kettledrums dominate this display of massed timpani and cymbals

tambourine. Furthermore, the percussionist has to master not one but several instruments to a professional level. Even something as 'simple' as striking a triangle is not so easy as the layman might think; we expect the characteristic 'ting' and get it if the instrument is struck near the top corner, but if it is hit in the middle of the bottom bar the sound is more of a 'clank' and much less delicate. Tuning the timpani used to be difficult, because the rest of the orchestra didn't stop while you did it and furthermore it had to be done almost inaudibly (only the player was supposed to hear); but now this is easier since there is a pedal device for tightening the drumhead and so raising the pitch. In lighter music with a regular beat, say in a musical show in the theatre, the percussionist must use his hands and at the same time play bass drum and clashed cymbals with pedals. After a two-hour show he looks forward to a hot bath; but the next night he has to face the same long-distance performance yet again.

Not many percussion performers play completely solo, though there is no real reason why they should not. It is a matter of what is available in the way of music. Edgard Varèse wrote a pioneering *Ionisation* for percussion in 1931, and the Welsh composer Daniel Jones composed a Timpani Sonata in 1947; but these were exceptions. Maybe the situation is changing. Pierre Boulez has written for percussion ensemble, and the Japanese percussionist Stomu Yamash'ta has had music written for him by Hans Werner Henze, the German composer, in which he must dash around his instrumental layout almost like a dancer. Yamash'ta has also produced music of his own with exotic titles like *As expanding as Red Buddha*.

Non-western musical cultures are often rich in percussion. No one who has heard the Balinese *gamelan* orchestra with its tuned gongs and drums is likely to forget a kind of sound which seems both fresh and timeless. In the meantime percussion instruments have a rich past and may look forward to a still richer future. In England at least, the student of percussion has the best available teaching. Most of the professors at the London music colleges are top symphony orchestra players.

The Modern Minstrels

10

At the beginning of this book we saw that an audience expects any performer to entertain them. The entertainment may be very simple, like juggling, or it may be something so profound and searching that we don't really use the word entertainment—say an intense drama like Shakespeare's *King Lear*. In both cases there is a paying audience, who will stay away if they do not like what is offered; tastes in entertainment may differ (anyway, why not enjoy different kinds on different occasions?) but the principle remains. Mozart once said about music that it first and foremost must 'please the listener' and that if it did not it was not music at all!

This leads us into what might be called 'artistic politics'. It was all very well for Mozart to say 'the listener', but today's listeners differ far more widely than those in Mozart's Vienna. The modern world has a wider distribution of money, and though the aristocrats and intellectuals may remain, their 'cultivated' tastes no longer count for much economically. In recent decades the big record companies have had to recognise that, like it or not, it is not 'serious' music that earns money but rock and folk styles. The twentieth-century composer Schoenberg once said scornfully that 'if it is for all, it is not art'; and, indeed, nobody puts on a concert of Schoenberg without expecting to lose money. What is so wonderful about that? People pay for Shakespeare and

'Duke' Ellington after a concert—playing the bass, however, rather than his own instrument, the piano

Beethoven, and nobody disputes the stature of those artists. 'One *ascends* to the public', said Fidel Castro, the Cuban leader—but he of course is a Marxist. Perhaps that idea is also a little too simple. To refer to people as 'the public' or 'the masses' can be rather insulting—perhaps politicians would like everyone to think and act alike, which would be very convenient for them! But after all, people are emphatically not mere units in a mass: on the contrary, they are individuals and have a right to be considered as such. A man's beliefs, loves—and musical tastes—are not identical to his neighbour's, any more than his fingerprints are. Why should they be?

It's time we got back to the entertainers. To earn a living they have to respond to what people really want. They can of course 'lead' an audience, but at the same time they must know how to reflect the changing moods and circumstances in which they entertain. And the entertainers who, throughout history, have remained closest to simpler tastes are the folk musicians who perform for ordinary working people who may have no interest in 'art' as such. Their music reflects the concerns of such people, and perhaps helps to make their lives more meaningful— and perhaps more bearable too.

Scott Joplin, who wrote the famous piano rag called *The Entertainer*, was a black American who emerged around 1900 from the minstrel tradition of an oppressed race. As early as the eighteenth century the *Virginia Gazette* had carried an advertisement offering for sale a horn-playing 'young healthy Negro fellow'. For slaves, music was an escape—sometimes much more than that as in the religious songs called spirituals. Joplin's mother played the banjo, the typical black folk instrument. But because slavery had ended and there was just a little economic freedom, her son had some musical training under white teachers and he learnt the piano. Joplin had his ambitions, and disappointments, as a 'serious' composer of opera, but it is for lazy, lilting ragtime piano that we remember him. Two who based their 'stride' style on ragtime were 'Jelly Roll' Morton and 'Fats' Waller. But by 1911 and *Alexander's Ragtime Band*, written by the Russian-born Irving Berlin, ragtime had joined a mainstream of white popular music.

Black musicians often joined together into small bands—cornet or clarinet, banjo, trombone, string bass, drums and perhaps piano. One cornet and trumpet player, Louis Armstrong (1900–1971), became a sort of jazz king in his long career. Born in a dingy, dangerous part of New Orleans of parents who were poor and barely literate, he came to music through his local church and then started listening to ragtime bands. A juvenile escapade landed him at twelve in a reformatory, but this turned out to be fortunate because its director helped him to learn the bugle, cornet and trumpet—and to read music as well. From the age of seventeen he played professionally in a band ... and did so for the rest of his career, playing (and singing) right up until 1970, the year before his death. He played trumpet in King Oliver's Creole Jazz Band; after that his 'own' bands included the 1927 Louis Armstrong and his Stompers and the 1947 Louis Armstrong All Stars. Some, like the All Stars, were big commercial touring bands; but there were also smaller groups like the Hot Five, Dixieland Seven and Hot Seven who were assembled for recordings. In the 1960s Armstrong toured the world as a kind of jazz ambassador. Even when over seventy he still played a two-week engagement with the All Stars at the Waldorf Astoria in New York. It was a life dedicated to music; but there was nothing in the least solemn about this kind of music-making. Blowing his 'horn', Louis said, was 'having *fun*'. His

Warm but undaunted, the legendary Louis Armstrong plays on

kind of art observes life keenly and above all *affirms* it in all its joys and sorrows. Louis Armstrong has been called the one jazz immortal, but his best epitaph may be these words of his own: 'My mama told me the first two words that I said were "Oh Yeah!"'—and it seems as though they have rubbed off on the world.'

The pianist and composer 'Duke' Ellington (1899–1974) belongs to Louis Armstrong's generation but was less straightforward as a musical personality. He played what was at times a kind of symphonic jazz using a large orchestra, impressive music often but perhaps without the directness of jazz style. For jazz style centres around solo performance and improvisation, individual talents and imaginations. The saxophonists Charlie Parker and John Coltrane, the trumpeters 'Dizzy' Gillespie and Miles Davis—these jazzmen make an impression above all as different musical personalities.

From the lighter jazz style of the 1930s and 1940s known as 'swing' developed a new, rhythmic style of popular music—rock n' roll. Reflecting the aspirations of a new post-war generation, the rock n' roll of the 1950s was lively and optimistic, and its musical style formed the model for most popular music since. Its star performers were usually singer-guitarists, the greatest of whom is Elvis Presley (1935–77), a cult figure whose records still reach the hit parade.

In the affluent 1960s pop music became more sophisticated, above all in the songs of the Beatles. Here again the guitar was important; it brought Paul McCartney into music after his mother died when he was fourteen. As his brother said, 'you lose a mother and you find a guitar . . . the minute he got the guitar he was lost, he didn't have time to eat or think about anything else, he played it on the lavatory, in the bath, everywhere.' He also more or less taught himself the trumpet and learned to pick out chords on the piano. Paul McCartney, together with John Lennon, George Harrison and Ringo Starr, the members of the Beatles group, had talent, drive, some luck and the ability to develop musically. But inevitably such strong individual personalities grew apart in time and went their own ways. In 1980 John Lennon's tragic death shocked the world. The Beatles fabulous success story is part of pop performance history. Other groups have followed their lead, encouraged by record companies and agents who dream of tapping more of the golden stream of super-success. And to 'make it' to the top, to seemingly boundless wealth, is still the daydream of many teenage rock fans. A British television play broadcast in 1980, called *The Boy with the Transistor Radio*, had as its central character a young school

The Rolling Stones and their lead singer Mick Jagger (born 1944). The group was formed around 1962 and soon nearly rivalled the Beatles in popularity; unlike the Liverpool group, the Stones have held together (though losing Brian Jones) and are still with us in 1981

leaver trying to live in an escape world of local radio and pop music, dreaming of a 'job in music' instead of the dreary warehouse life that he was offered. At the end the author, Willy Russell, showed him unskilfully and in increasing frustration strumming away at a guitar in his bedroom.

The pop performer's kind of entertainment can be escapist. The smooth patter of the disc jockey and the non-stop music belted out from his array of turntables dazzles and excites his young audience. It is an unreal world, but it attracts by pushing aside dullness, worry and drab surroundings. Some pop music is unashamedly commercial; and certain performers regard their work as sheer rubbish which is greedily accepted by a 'public' they despise. But that is not the whole story, and there are many others who shun the easily-digested commercial style and produce genuinely original music. Many work in kinds of advanced music that cannot be labelled jazz, pop or 'art' music, using elements from all three and mixing free improvisation with composition, electric and acoustic instruments with synthesized sound.

There are alarming elements to be found in the pop music scene of recent years. Several leading performers have died at least partially as a result of using drugs—the jazz saxophonist Charlie Parker, the guitarist Jimi Hendrix, Brian Jones of the Rolling Stones, and 'Sid Vicious' of The Sex Pistols. Punk rock style—like that of Vicious himself—is aggressive, even violent, and expresses extreme social disenchantment. The performer, as we have seen throughout this book, has always reflected the attitudes of his public, and also had power over it. One hopes that such power may be used responsibly.

Whatever our attitude to pop music, we cannot ignore its power and its wide appeal. For all its commercial elements, it is the folk music of our day and a vital expression of our age—possibly more so than any other music. Meanwhile, the popular performer remains a power in the land, more perhaps today than ever before. The wealth of the Beatles—or of the pianist Liberace—symbolizes their star status. Liberace once made a famous remark about those critics who slated his performance as tasteless and vulgar—'I cried all the way to the bank'. But

Liberace's style is actually 'homey' compared to that of the punk rockers. He appeals, in fact, to an older audience. But the rock audiences of today will be the middle-aged parents of the next generation. Who will be the performers who most answer to their needs, the stars of the year 2000? The question is unanswerable. But the essentials of human nature do not change. We must leave the future to look after itself. In the meantime a performer's job is to do what he can, as well as he can, and for as long as he can.

Sting, lead singer with Police, one of Britain's New Wave bands which has achieved international stardom

99

11 Jerry Harrison
Rock Musician

The Talking Heads were once grouped with New York's punk rock movement, but in the last few years they have emerged as an adventurous and innovative band whose 'sound' defies simple labels. Originality is the band's keynote and is a quality highly prized by their keyboard player and guitarist, Jerry Harrison.

At an early age, Jerry took piano lessons and learned to play the saxophone (like his father who had played sax in a jazz band). The guitar came later, only about six years ago in fact. Jerry's real knowledge and ability came from performing experience with different bands and from listening to records. He believes this sort of informal learning can be more important than formal training and says: 'Classical training can sometimes hinder you. You don't think of making things up on the spot, you don't think of expressing yourself. You shouldn't *just* sit around playing Liszt or Bartók or anybody. You must try to figure them out and copy them, and then try to make up things of your own.' He believes there is a similarity with writers in this respect: 'At Harvard, they were trained to be so critical that their sense of creation didn't come anywhere near their level of criticism. They learned to pick apart people like James Joyce and T. S. Eliot and after that they found it hard to get started themselves; after that how could any of them possibly write anything they liked? Look at all these bands who learn how to play everybody else's songs. They end up writing songs that are amalgamations of other people's. That was one of the great things about punk music, people would pick up guitars and express themselves with whatever means they had. It didn't really matter if it wasn't sophisticated; the intensity of the expression's what counted.'

In the early seventies, Jerry played in a group called Modern Lovers, whom he describes as 'precursors of the New Wave and the Punk'. At that date, however, this sort of music was totally unfashionable. 'We were really alone, there wasn't any music much like ours in the world. I think there's a sort of chain which can go: the Velvet Underground, the Stooges and then the Modern Lovers. It had nothing to do with the blues or anything like that. It was a whole counter sense of rhythm. In some ways all the things that came out later, owed a debt to that music. It sort of exploded, with all the bands from the Ramones to the Sex Pistols . . .'

Jerry Harrison

As with anything new, though, there are drawbacks, as Jerry points out. 'We starved for a long time. It's great to be original but it's really something else when you have to convince every audience— *every one*—that the whole style of music is even worth listening to. All rock music is an awful lot of work. You have to move your own equipment the whole time. You start at two or four in the afternoon and you load everything into some vehicle, drive wherever you're going. Then you always find you've got to set up on the fifth floor of a place or get down a ladder into a basement. Then you play for several hours, pack it all up, drive, unload—for about $25 (£10).

'Then we got all this record company interest. We used to sort of save up and once in a while the record companies would take us out to eat and we would just stuff ourselves, and then we wouldn't eat for a bit, then we'd wait for the next record company to take us out. But eventually we broke up because we started tearing apart at each other from being together too long. And then what happened was that a record we had made as a demo tape was released about four years after it'd been made.'

Jerry had joined the Modern Lovers while he was

101

still at Harvard, and had dropped out during his final year. Before that he had played in bands all through school, performing at dances and football games. Despite always performing and also doing an extra-curricular course in music while he was at Harvard, it was not until he joined the Modern Lovers that Jerry really decided that he could try to make a living at music.

After the band split up he stopped performing and taught music for a while, even worked briefly for a computer company. 'Finally I quit. It was driving me crazy. I was interested in computers, but those people lived and breathed them. I just didn't have the obsessive interests they had. And then I thought, "What am I doing fooling around with something I'm only *mildly* interested in?" It was a good lesson.' The commercial success of the Talking Heads has not warped Jerry's belief in the importance of doing something you believe in. 'The glamour and all that is not particularly rewarding. If you feel great about what you are doing, then obviously the fact that people appreciate it is great. But if you're not happy without that then you start doing everything for the wrong reason. I'm not a big believer in saying there are right and wrong reasons, but I think if you do it for the money or for superficial reasons then you'll end up not making the right artistic decisions.'

Jerry joined the Talking Heads in 1977 just before the band made their first album, *Talking Heads: 77.* 'They made a single after I met them but before I joined them. But I played on the first album. I joined at a very nice time. I didn't have to put up with the sort of intense poverty you have to go through at the beginning. I felt like I'd already gone through that.' Shortly afterwards the Heads went on a European tour, opening for the Ramones. 'We really went over well, and there wasn't the pressure of being the headliner so it was just a lot of fun. I think in some ways the very early stages of a band are really exciting because it's so far to go and you can really see the changes, though naturally you look back on things and make them out to be better than they were. Maybe next year I'll look back and say "Oh, this year was the best".'

In 1978 *More Songs About Buildings and Food* was

released and in 1979 their most popular album to
date, *Fear of Music*, appeared. With every album
their reputation and popularity has grown, so that
now they have what Jerry calls 'all the para-
phernalia'. This includes a manager, an agent, an
accountant, a lawyer, and of course, roadies. Obviously it is expensive, but it is also a form of
protection from the pressures of the rock world and
the problems that accompany financial success, not
that Jerry allows it to spoil him: 'I guess it means that
I don't always think about how I'm going to pay for
the next cup of coffee. That's what success feels like
more than anything. I don't feel like I'm rich or
anything, I just feel like I'm not obsessed by how I'm
going to pay my next rent. I went so many years when
every bill was such a disaster.'

Jerry (left) and David
Byrne of The Talking
Heads in concert

103

Jerry's clear-headed appreciation of the money side of the rock world is combined with an affection for the openness of the business. He finds this contrasts strongly with the hypocrisy of the art world in which he once considered a career, and says, 'They sort of pretend that it's all like it was in the seventeenth century, that it's pure and high culture, but that's all wrong. There's no question that people like Andy Warhol were really intelligently promoted. At least in rock n' roll all the unpleasant qualities are out front, and I appreciate that. It's true that people make money off of records, but it's more natural. There has to be a form of distribution and obviously some people do that for what they can get out of it, but that's O.K. with me. In rock n' roll there's no single thing of value, it's all duplicates and all basically affordable. You can buy a record for $5 or $6 and in that way it's more a proletarian sort of art form.'

Despite the advantages of reaching a broader public through recording, Jerry finds he gets most pleasure from performing live. It is gruelling work and of course there is less chance of a band getting exactly the sound they want, but it has its own rewards. 'It's very thrilling, particularly if you feel good about what you're performing and if you feel that the audience will be excited by it. There is a real conduction of energy, a real interplay between the performer and the audience. An audience can bring out the best in a performer and vice versa. When those moments come there's hardly anything that matches them.'

Lastly, Jerry has this advice for young musicians: 'Try to figure out what quality is original when you play. Work on that, concentrate on that, develop it and don't worry that you can't sound like somebody else. Not that you shouldn't work on technical points, but try to come up with a sense of what a musician's style is, what he is excited by the most. Never put off trying to create and trying to make things up, because that's what it's all about. And don't do it because you want to be famous, or for the glamour you see in the future. Do it because you enjoy it.'

Practical Matters

12

Choosing an Instrument

Let's suppose that you have decided that you want to learn an instrument. A word of caution is necessary even at this stage. Almost everyone would *in theory* like to be a musical performer—but that's not quite enough. Similarly, I would like to be a good footballer or an expert chess player, but in fact I lack the necessary physical and intellectual attributes, and furthermore I am not really committed to either of these pursuits. To take up a musical instrument successfully you need a real interest in music—and talent, too, though talent and interest often go together. It is going to take time, patience and determination to get results. How much time depends on how ambitious you are, of course, and you don't need to devote yourself exclusively to music unless you want to be a professional. Even then, not quite exclusively; that would make you too narrow to be a complete artist. But there's got to be dedication. Remember what Paul McCartney's brother said about Paul and his guitar—'he didn't have time to eat or think about anything else.' You've got to love music and to want to express that love through your instrument.

Usually the choice of an instrument comes through your own musical taste. If you like guitar music, and maybe some particular player, you will want to make your music on the guitar. Or you may live in a house

The complex keywork of the bassoon needs a dexterous player with a fairly large hand

where someone plays the trumpet or the piano, and want to do the same. That is the lead to follow: have a go at what attracts you. If you show any kind of aptitude for the instrument, you have at least made a start as a performer. And if you don't do so well? If you are still keen, you may find that you have greater aptitude for some other instrument—so try another!

Choosing a Teacher

At this point it is vital to get some guidance. Without it you are going to waste time, get frustrated and discouraged, and possibly give up altogether. If you take up an instrument at school, then your school will choose your teacher for you. There are advantages in this: the teacher will be properly qualified and experienced, you may be able to borrow an instrument until the time comes to buy your own, and you will probably have the stimulus of working with other beginners, or playing in groups and even orchestras. On the other hand, lessons may not be given on an individual basis; they may be short; or

Teaching the violin by the Suzuki method, where pupils can start at five or younger

they may be at an awkward time of day when you (and perhaps the teacher) are tired and unreceptive. Playing the violin in groups and then leaving the instrument at school—never practising alone at home—is not a recipe for progress.

Suppose, on the other hand, that you choose a private teacher. You will probably pay more for your lessons, but they may be longer and should be more individual in approach; you will know where your teacher lives and be able to contact him between lessons in an emergency—if your clarinet keys fall off or your violin bridge collapses. He may be more of a specialist than a teacher at school. The way most people find a private teacher is by personal recommendation from someone else, either a pupil or a parent. That usually works well; but the teacher-to-pupil relationship is a special one and it is possible that what suits your neighbour does not suit you. The best teachers, though, respond differently to the individual personalities, talents and needs of their pupils, and should be able to fit themselves to your requirements. (Don't forget that a good teacher *does* know your needs. Sometimes progress is slow because the pupil is determined that he knows best!) Failing personal recommendation, the best way of finding a private teacher in Britain is to get the booklet called *Professional Register of Private*

Teachers of Music from the Incorporated Society of Musicians in London. This is a professional body and its members are qualified musicians; the Private Teachers' Section is open only to experienced teachers and you may have confidence in the names included. Fees, of course, will vary according to the teacher's standing and the level of tuition; don't forget that he has to maintain a studio and his instruments. In 1981, the minimum fee you must expect to pay for your lessons is about £6.60 (or $15.00) per hour, but if you are a beginner receiving a 30-minute or 40-minute lesson you will pay correspondingly less.

Perhaps you find that there are several teachers in your area offering tuition in your chosen instrument. Most of them have various letters after their names. A diploma is important—and a teachers' diploma at that. In Britain, look for initials such as LRAM, ARCM, GRSM, ARMCM, ARNCM, LGSM, LTCL—and, for organ teachers, FRCO or ARCO. These represent diploma qualifications from various colleges of music in Great Britain, and there are others which are also valid. In America the relevant initials for organ teachers are AAGO and FAGO and other reliable music teachers will probably belong

Yehudi Menuhin and some of the exceptionally gifted young musicians who are pupils at the Menuhin School which he founded in 1962 at Stoke d'Abernon near London

to National Associations or Federations, have qualifications from conservatories like Juilliard's in New York, or university degrees. But in either country do not necessarily be swayed in your choice by a university degree in music (like BA or BMus). This denotes a breadth of study which may be useful, but if you are starting on the cello it is much more important that your teacher knows and cares about cello playing than that he knows about music history. If you are examination-minded, in Britain you may choose a teacher whose pupils sit the exams of the Associated Board of the Royal Schools of Music and are generally successful (Merit marks, not bare passes!); but you will only gather this sort of information by word of mouth since few teachers publish these things. The local competitive festivals of music will also provide useful clues: if someone plays imaginatively as well as accurately it is likely that his teacher develops musicianship as well as technique.

Your teacher, once you have one, will advise on the choice of an instrument. The safest advice is to buy the best you can afford. This is a counsel of perfection, you may think. But a good instrument can always be resold, and if well looked after will increase in value. The idea that a poor instrument is 'suitable for beginners' is utterly false. Pianos, in particular, sometimes go beyond repair and deserve to be thrown out or used simply as furniture. It is very difficult to make progress on any instrument with poor action, or which is out of tune.

Colleges of Music

Imagine that you have had seven or eight years of experience as an instrumentalist. You have perhaps passed the Associated Board Grade VIII examination with a Distinction (at least 130 marks out of 150) or a very good Merit. Perhaps you have an 'A' Level GCE in Music also. If you are as musical as this, you may well play another instrument, or sing, up to Grade VI or so. You may have played in a school orchestra— perhaps a county youth orchestra or even (the ambition of every young performer) the National Youth Orchestra of Great Britain, that of the European Community or one of several in the United

A concert at the Royal College of Music, London, in 1978. Sir David Willcocks directs his students in a performance of Walton's oratorio *Belshazzar's Feast*

States. If you are an organist, you may be regularly deputizing in the local church or even a cathedral. As a pianist, you may have carried off prizes in county competitive festivals, or played as a recitalist on your local radio station; you may even aspire to perform in the Young Musician of the Year competition organized by BBC Television. Details of orchestras, competitions, and many other useful matters are given in the *British Music Yearbook* published annually by A & C Black in London and in *Musical American*, a magazine published by ABC Leisure Magazines Inc. Both are kept in most public libraries in their respective countries.

If you have reached this high standard—which only a few do—then the full-time study of music is probably your next stage. The various schools or colleges of music offer the advanced tuition you now require, and from these you will emerge qualified for a career as a professional performer. There are grants to help you through your student years—the course will last three or four years—and scholarships too. You will have to give an audition, playing to college teachers, to get in. After that, you are in the hands of the institution itself. Demands will be made on your technique and your interpretative abilities that you may not have anticipated; for you will be facing up to the greatest and most demanding music in the repertory of your instrument. You will find that there are other students who seem more gifted than

110

yourself; but don't worry, they may be thinking the same about you! In any case—let's face it—you are preparing for one of the most competitive professions that exist today. For whereas a qualified doctor or lawyer or accountant can be almost certain of a job, the qualified pianist (or, to a lesser extent, orchestral instrumentalist) is far from being as well placed. There are at most twenty pianists in Britain today who earn a living exclusively from concert playing, and although there are probably that number doing the same in New York there are very few anywhere else.

Competitions

And now, at last, you are a qualified professional: you have graduated from your college of music. What next? Well, the ideal way to get a 'launch' for your career is to win a major competition. There are several of these, some carrying great status like the Carl Flesch Violin Competition or the Karajan Conductors' Competition in Berlin; in Britain the Leeds International Piano Competition has great importance; and in America there is the Leventritt Memorial Competition in New York and the Van Cliburn Competition in Fort Worth, Texas. Success here—even a second or third prize—may carry with it guaranteed engagements and probably a recording contract as well. You have now got pretty well to the top; all you have to do is to stay there! At this stage you need little further advice from me—except to keep your head, work hard, never take success for granted and go on loving (and learning) music.

The Louisiana-born pianist Van Cliburn won the Moscow Tchaikovsky Competition in 1958 at the age of 23 and is seen here receiving bouquets of flowers following his final concert in the Moscow Conservatoire

The Performer's Career

Failing the spectacular success of a competition win, the performer sets about things more quietly. The British Incorporated Society of Musicians published in 1978 a booklet called *Managing your Career: Advice for Young Performers*. It was compiled with the help of the singer Ian Wallace and the singer-guitarist Leonard Pearcey and is full of good, practical advice. You are not told to play well—it is assumed that you do this already! Instead you are advised to look ahead and plan your career, using the talents you possess to their fullest advantage; to be businesslike, charging realistic fees, answering letters promptly, and fulfilling your engagements with the minimum of fuss; to advertise yourself sensibly; to behave well during the hospitality session offered after a concert, and so on. Matters such as self-promotion and agents also are discussed here. In short, an agent will take you on to his books only if he thinks you will earn him money—his percentage of your fee. But it is worth remembering that he too must help you by getting you engagements you would not otherwise have had: the established agents are the hardest to join, but these are the ones who will offer you the best jobs.

There are many other matters to consider. Among these are broadcasting and recording, unions or other professional organizations, the insurance of instruments and self-employed pension schemes. You will need to be able to write an invoice and perhaps use a typewriter—or if you're really successful, employ a secretary! Secretary or no, sooner or later you will need an accountant. But an accountant's fees are not alarming—and these, like many other things from necessary travel to instrument maintenance, can be set against Income Tax as a legitimate business expense. Leonard Pearcey's article in the 1980 *British Music Yearbook*, 'Making a Start: The Young Performer', has some useful ideas and information. The essential thing is to take an active attitude to your career, not to sit about waiting for the world to come to you. It's difficult, sometimes, for a sensitive artist: but it's necessary.

School music under ideal conditions: a string quartet rehearses at Christ's Hospital, near Horsham in Sussex

Envoi

As a young performer, whether a school-age beginner or a qualified professional, you are fortunate; music gives you joy and the potential for sharing that joy with others. It's demanding; of course it is; and yet the hard work is not really 'work', but pleasure. It is sometimes lonely—during those long hours of practice—and yet when you play to others you communicate at a profound level and by so doing you can enrich their lives. Music is like a friend who will never desert you. At a time when many established social values are being questioned, the art which you have chosen to serve remains something to which people increasingly turn as a solace and a strength in a difficult, changing world. Yours, then, is a noble vocation. By practising music, whether as a pastime or as a profession, you make the world a better and a happier place.

Acknowledgments

The illustrations are reproduced by kind permission of the following:
H. Roger Viollet 2, 6, 12, 27; Nigel Luckhurst 3, 61; The Mansell
Collection 5, 14, 15, 17, 18, 21, 45, 47; BBC Hulton Picture Library 9, 13,
20, 30, 69, 85; Peter Newark's Historical Pictures 10; Archiv für Kunst
und Geschichte, Berlin 23, 24, 25, 28, Zoë Dominic 33, 36, 37; Ronald
Grant 40; Clive Barda 49,55, 57, 58, 60, 64, 65, 68, 82–3, 87, 90, 91, 106,
107; Novosti Press Agency 51; Siegfried Lauterwasser/EMI Limited 52;
Eileen Preston 54, 73; Rex Features LTD 70–71, 96; Alan J. Wood,
Photographer 80; Sovfoto/East Foto 86, 111; Culver Pictures, Inc. 88;
Central Press Photos Ltd 94; David Redfern Photography (Photo:
Richard Aaron) 97, (Photo: Mike Prior) 99, (Photo: Gary Gershoff) 103;
Brech-Einzig Limited 108, 113; Jennie Walton 110.

The author is also pleased to acknowledge the many fruitful ideas that
he gleaned from an excellent BBC radio series broadcast in 1980:
Music for a Living, produced from Manchester by Gillian Hush.